T0154220

WHO IS THE BUDDHA?

Also by Sangharakshita

Books on Buddhism
The Eternal Legacy
A Survey of Buddhism
The Ten Pillars of Buddhism
The Three Jewels

Edited Seminars and Lectures
The Bodhisattva Ideal
Buddha Mind
The Buddha's Noble Eightfold Path
The Buddha's Victory
Buddhism for Today – and Tomorrow
Creative Symbols of Tantric Buddhism
The Drama of Cosmic Enlightenment
The Essence of Zen
A Guide to the Buddhist Path
Human Enlightenment
The Inconceivable Emancipation
Living with Awareness
Living with Kindness
Know Your Mind
The Meaning of Conversion in Buddhism
New Currents in Western Buddhism
Ritual and Devotion in Buddhism
The Taste of Freedom
Tibetan Buddhism: An Introduction
Transforming Self and World
What Is the Dharma?
What Is the Sangha?
Who Is the Buddha?
Wisdom Beyond Words

Essays
Alternative Traditions
Crossing the Stream
Forty-Three Years Ago
From Genesis to the Diamond Sutra
The FWBO and 'Protestant Buddhism'
Going for Refuge
The History of My Going for Refuge
The Priceless Jewel
Was the Buddha a Bhikkhu?

Memoirs and Letters
Facing Mount Kanchenjunga
In the Sign of the Golden Wheel
Precious Teachers
Moving Against the Stream
The Rainbow Road
Travel Letters
Through Buddhist Eyes

Art and Poetry
The Call of the Forest and Other Poems
Complete Poems 1941–1994
In the Realm of the Lotus
The Religion of Art

Miscellaneous
Ambedkar and Buddhism
Peace is a Fire
A Stream of Stars

SANGHARAKSHITA

WHO IS THE BUDDHA?

WINDHORSE PUBLICATIONS

Published by Windhorse Publications
169 Mill Road
Cambridge
CB1 3AN
United Kingdom

© Sangharakshita 1994
Reprinted 1995, 2012
Second edition 2002

Printed by CPI Group (UK) Ltd, Croydon, CR0 4YY

The cover shows the Buddha, Tibet, 18th century
courtesy of the Trustees of the Victoria and Albert Museum
Cover design   Dhammarati
Text illustrations   Varaprabha

British Library Cataloguing in Publication Data
A catalogue record for this book is available from the British Library

ISBN   1 899579 81 6
(first edition 0 904766 24 1)

CONTENTS

About the Author

Sangharakshita was born Dennis Lingwood in South London, in 1925. Largely self-educated, he developed an interest in the cultures and philosophies of the East as a teenager, and realized that he was a Buddhist.

The Second World War took him to India, where he stayed on to become a Buddhist monk. After studying under leading teachers from the major Buddhist traditions, he went on to teach and write exten - sively. He also played a key part in the revival of Buddhism in India, particularly through his work among followers of Dr B.R. Ambedkar.

After twenty years in India, he returned to England to establish the Friends of the Western Buddhist Order (FWBO) in 1967, and the Western Buddhist Order (called Trailokya Bauddha Mahasangha in India) in 1968. Since that time, he has devoted much of his time to speaking , writing, and travel, and his depth of experience and clarity of thought have been appreciated throughout the world.

The FWBO is now an international Buddhist movement with over sixty centres on five continents. In recent years Sangharakshita has handed on most of his responsibilities to his senior disciples in the Order. From his base in Birmingham, he is now focusing on personal contact with people, and on his writing.

Editors' Preface

THE STORY OF THE BUDDHA'S LIFE is one that has appealed to the Western imagination ever since scholars first brought it to the notice of the European reading public. Sir Edwin Arnold's extended poem on the subject, *The Light of Asia*, enjoyed a considerable vogue at the beginning of the twentieth century; Richard Wagner would almost certainly have made an opera about the Buddha, had he lived long enough to do so; Hermann Hesse wrote a hugely successful novel about him; and today it is the turn of the film makers. None of these treatments are – or, in the case of Wagner, were to be – straightforward biographies. It is as if the academics and historians had opened the door on a subject that essentially lay beyond their competence. For a great many people, even those who have not considered the possibility of becoming Buddhists themselves, the Buddha is the archetype of the seeker after truth. As such he perhaps represents for them an aspect of themselves that needs to be addressed at a deeper level than that reached by bald historical records.

The religious inheritance of the West can sometimes seem muddied with acrimony and political strife, and the mysteries of religion a matter of baffled exasperation rather than devout wonder. By comparison, the image of the Buddha with which everyone is familiar seems a figure of unfathomable knowledge and compassion. Its message is not strident or defensive. It does not call forth fear or guilt. Instead, it triggers off a subtle perplexity in ourselves, a questioning of our deepest assumptions – about what is possible, about what can be known and what cannot be known, about what a human being can become. We may recognize in it something in ourselves that we have not perhaps taken into account; and the belief may stir in us that such knowledge and serenity might be available to ourselves.

But the mood is easily shaken off. What seems unfathomable may simply be oriental inscrutability. The inconceivable is perhaps just impenetrable. Is he imperturbable or just impassive? Serene or just tranquillized? Perhaps there is nothing at all behind the mask.

Who is the Buddha? Is he just a distinctive fashion accessory for our times? Is he just a great marketing concept for advertising campaigns? Or might it just be possible that he really did isolate and transcend the riddle of existence, that he really did lay down a clear guide to how we can do the same for ourselves – that, in short, he really does represent what we ultimately aspire to? When we ask 'Who is the Buddha?' we are also perhaps asking a question altogether closer to home.

It is not, after all, an academic or historical or 'human interest' question, like 'Who *was* the Buddha?' In ordinary terms 'Who *is* the Buddha?' does not make sense. We would not ask, say, 'Who *is* Napoleon?' Generally, the present tense is used to refer to ostensibly dead individuals only if they have divine status. One might say, 'Who is Jesus?' for example, if one believed that he sits at the right hand of God and exists as a living presence in the hearts of his followers. But the Buddha is not God, nor *a* god, nor does he issue from God. So he is not existent in simple divine terms. And yet the question addressed by this book is one that has exercised the minds of Buddhists from the time the Buddha appeared right up to the present day. In the end, it is a *koan* – that is to say, it cannot be answered in its own terms; it requires us to change ourselves before we can answer it.

One of the most mysterious titles in the modern publishing world is *Who's Who*. It is, of course, a sort of identity parade of significant figures in public life. But it is plainly evident that this compendium does not, in fact, set out to tell us who anybody is in a way that makes much sense to us today. Generally speaking, we are nowadays much less comfortable with setting out our identity in this fashion than people were in the past. Who we are and what is our purpose in life are questions which people in the past had settled for them. Most people had neither the time nor the energy to dispute the answers given to them. But today our sure if limited sense of identity, as well as the closed systems of belief which secure it, are slipping away at all levels of society. We do question things. We don't want pat answers.

It is the Buddha's direct confrontation of the existential crisis faced by the individual which makes him easily accessible to contemporary modes of thought. An attitude of doubt, experimentation, and questioning marks the whole of the Buddha's career before he became Enlightened. And his subsequent teaching at no point cuts short the spiritual quest with premature conceptual resolutions, divine revelation, or doctrinal imperatives. The only difference between the Buddha's quest and our own is that he had to find his way without clues or guidance. In asking 'Who is the Buddha?' we are simply undertaking the Buddha's interrogation of reality for ourselves. The quest remains our own because this interrogation of reality is also an interrogation of ourselves at the deepest level.

It will be clear by now that the question 'Who is the Buddha?' is not going to receive in this book a reply that bears any relation to a *Who's Who* entry, or even to a spiritual biography. The author's concern in the following pages is to lay bare, so far as this is possible, the roots of the Buddha's essential identity as an *Enlightened* human being.

The opening chapter is, in some ways, the most ambitious in the book. Within a few pages it sets out a coherent overview of the Buddhist perspective on the universe within which the Buddha can be recognized for who he is. That is to say, it provides a window for Westerners to look through the Buddhist window on the universe. At the same time, Sangharakshita scrupulously avoids the danger of confusing one window for the other. The idea, for example, that Buddhism is a scientific religion is a plausible and attractive one for many people. There are facets to both disciplines – in terms of attitude and procedures – that make it seem as if the Buddha was a kind of scientist, applying scientific method to the spiritual life. But as Sangharakshita explains, such a synthesis misrepresents science and sells Buddhism short.

In the Buddha's early life, before he became the Buddha, we gain an acquaintance with some of the elements that made up his character. We get to know the circumstances Prince Siddhārtha grew up in and the use he made of those circumstances to engineer the most ambitious project of which a human being is capable. This period in his life – the way to Enlightenment – is a poetic mix of legend and real human touches. One may find his background is quite a curious one for the

founder of the kind of religion that people usually consider Buddhism
to be.

Because it concerns a human being like ourselves *before* he became
the Buddha, his early life is a fertile source of inspiration and guidance
for us. But the teachings that Sangharakshita uncovers from this ancient
story are almost shockingly down-to-earth. One could say that he
brings the issues that Siddhārtha faced into our own living rooms.

There is a particular element in Siddhārtha's make-up, however,
which is so fundamental that it almost always gets overlooked. This is
his heroism, which has a whole chapter to itself. His deeply martial
spirit, which propelled him all the way to Enlightenment, will no doubt
come as a surprise to some. The subject of the succeeding chapter will
be even more of a surprise, perhaps, though it is equally fundamental
to the nature of Buddhahood. As a Buddha he is above and beyond all
other beings, up to and including Godhead; and yet upon becoming
Enlightened, almost the first thing he considered was who or what he
should worship. Why? And what are the implications for us?

After his Enlightenment, the Buddha devoted the whole of his life to
teaching. Being Enlightened clearly involved a wish to communicate.
But this is not the place for a detailed exposition of everything he
taught. As far as this aspect of his life is concerned Sangharakshita again
takes a slightly unusual angle. He examines not so much what he
communicated as the nature of his communication – *how* he communicated. Included in this chapter is a brief guide through the maze of the
Buddhist scriptures, in which the Buddha speaks with an astoundingly
rich variety of voices.

On the other hand, there is no understanding of who the Buddha is
without some idea of the content of the realization which made him
what he is. Furthermore, as that realization was the culmination of
many previous lives, the subject of karma and rebirth also needs to be
understood. In the West, the idea of reincarnation tends to get quite
obfuscated, so it needs looking at with some care. Certainly, the Buddhist conception of karma and rebirth cannot be dismissed until it is fully
understood, which as Sangharakshita's patient exposition demon-
strates, is by no means the simple matter it is often taken to be.

As for the Buddha's 'death', this is traditionally associated with meditation – particularly, of course, with meditation on impermanence and
death. By describing some of the key contemplative practices of the
Buddhist tradition Sangharakshita leads us towards distinguishing, in
a very graphic way, between death in the usual sense of the word and

the 'death' of the Buddha. In conclusion, the final chapter makes clear what we can say about who the Buddha is and what we have to find out for ourselves through our own spiritual practice and experience.

Having given a short account of the structure of the book, we should point out that its unity has been manufactured in the process of editing. It is by no means a single composition. It has, in fact, been put together from a dozen different and disparate lectures. Sangharakshita has always devoted as much time as he can to writing, but of the substantial list of literary works to his name, a growing number are the fruit of his work as a speaker and seminar leader. His gifts in this direction have long been recognized, and the extraordinarily rich store of reflection and insight into Buddhism held in the recordings of his talks and seminars are slowly being released in book form. The present work has been edited from twelve lectures selected from an archive of over three hundred.

This book is not, therefore, just another book on Buddhism, laboured over in front of a word-processor. It is the record of a Buddhist communicating himself to others, just as the Buddha's teaching is the record made by others of the Buddha's own communication of himself. What Sangharakshita says is informed by half a century of contemplating the Buddha's teaching and practising it for himself – as well as being backed up by very wide reading and an even wider experience of life, in both the East and the West. It is Sangharakshita's strength, in a field which has been much overgrown in recent years by woolly mysticism, wild speculative theories, and colourful psycho-babble, that he is able to make the Buddha's message relevant to us without falsifying it. Given at widely differing times in the last twenty-five years, and delivered to widely differing audiences, these talks have been edited quite radically – pruned back and in some cases interwoven with material from other talks on the same theme. But our hope is that the result still preserves some of the freshness and urgency of those live encounters.

Jinananda and Vidyadevi
Spoken Word Project
London
November 1993

1

The Evolution of a Buddha

'WHO IS THE BUDDHA?' This question has always been crucial to the Buddhist quest. Through it, Buddhists determine their ideal, their goal in life, and their whole spiritual path. It is as an essentially practical question in this sense that it appears as the title of this book. We shall be examining, through the following chapters, some of the significant events in the Buddha's life, as it occurred 2,500 years ago. However, the question 'Who is the Buddha?' is not answered by a simple biography – at least not in a very helpful sense. Besides, matters of historical fact are not fundamental issues to Buddhists. Scholars continue to dispute over whether certain details in the various traditional records may or may not be regarded as true statements of what actually happened. But for those who follow in the Buddha's footsteps the facts of his life, such as they are, are secondary to their significance as a guide to the spiritual path. Many biographies of the Buddha, both popular and scholarly, have appeared before now, and some of these are both informative and inspiring. But our approach here is different. Our aim is the specific one of reflecting on the Buddhist conception of who the Buddha is.

We are therefore taking each of the major elements in the Buddha's career as the starting point for a consideration of the ideal and goal of Buddhism as he exemplifies it, and as we also can strive after it. To begin with, however, it will be useful to get an idea of the spiritual context within which the man, Siddhārtha Gautama, became the Buddha. That is, the Buddha cannot be recognized for what he is except from within the context of Buddhism itself. From the Buddhist point of view the Buddha did not arise from nowhere. It is true that Buddhism as we know it starts with the Buddha. But he did not invent or create the Dharma, the truth around which Buddhism developed. He discovered it – or rather he rediscovered it. The Buddha takes his place at the centre – or at the culmination – of a vast pattern or system of spiritual hierarchies. To know who he is we also have to know, in a manner of speaking, where he is. If we cannot get some measure of the scale of the Buddha's achievement against our own human experience, the question 'Who is the Buddha?' cannot realistically be addressed at all. Therefore, not only do we need to take in as comprehensive a view as we can of the Buddhist 'scheme of things', but we should also try to see Buddhism itself in the most far-reaching perspective. 'Who is the Buddha?' is another way of saying 'Where does Buddhism propose to lead us?' To answer it we need to have some idea of where we are now – and even of how we came to be here. Before we look at where the human quest ends, we should also, perhaps, look back at its origins, where it begins.

In the beginning, we may say, life was a mystery. That, at least, was how it seemed to primitive humanity. Without formulating it as such, people felt, as though in the blood, that life was strange, incomprehensible: a mystery. Then later on, though still during humankind's unrecorded past, people began consciously, explicitly, to think about life. Our ancestors apprehended that they were – without knowing how or why – in the midst of what seemed to be a strange and even hostile world, surrounded by all sorts of things which they could not understand or control. In the morning they saw the sun rise, and in the evening they saw it set. But why the sun rose and why it set, and what happened to it when darkness fell, they just did not know. Sometimes there were great storms – the world grew dark, rain fell, thunder seemed to crack open the earth and the sky would be lit up by an intermittent and terrible glare. But what caused these disturbances no one could tell. The days might be long and warm, or they might be short and freezing, but why they should be so was, again, a mystery. Eventually, they discovered that they could strike two stones together to make fire – and here was another mystery.

Sometimes people felt acutely miserable, and their bodies were racked with terrible pains. Why? They didn't know. And sometimes something even stranger happened. Someone would be found lying on the ground, quite still. Usually it would be an old person, but not always; and sometimes it would be a child. When you called them they did not answer. You saw that their eyes were fixed and staring, but they did not recognize you. When you drew near, when you placed your fingers near their nostrils, you discovered that they no longer breathed. When you touched them you found that their flesh was cold and hard. If you left them where they were then sooner or later you noticed a dreadful smell coming from them. And this was the greatest mystery of all.

Almost as soon as these mysteries arose, it seems, they would have been named and given a place in a larger pattern of meaning whereby people could make some sense of their lives. And this world view – the particular view of the world held in any one society or social group – would satisfy people for perhaps a very long time indeed. But eventually some inconsistencies would appear, some aspects of the world or of themselves would be discovered that could not be explained within that system, that would not fit into it. Some people would then simply choose to muddle along with the old system, making a few adjustments here and there, while others would dismantle the whole apparatus and start again from a completely different governing principle.

What has changed today is that people have now, in most places in the world, a very considerable range of world views – of beliefs, myths, and philosophies – to choose from and learn from. This can only be a good thing. As Kipling shrewdly demanded of an earlier, nationalistic age, 'What should they know of England who only England know?'[1] You can hardly be said to know your own culture if you have nothing to compare it with, and the same goes for anything else one wants to know: knowledge is essentially comparison. You cannot really understand even your own religion except in relation to other religions. Of course, one hasn't always had the information one needed to make these comparisons. Fifty years ago you hardly ever heard another religion apart from Christianity even mentioned – you were not given to understand such religions existed at all. But today all this has changed. Kipling's *aperçu* now seems almost a truism, and one finds one can learn a great deal about one's own faith from studying other systems of belief. Things we would have taken for granted in the past we can now see for what they are by comparison with different things of the same nature. And one appreciates and understands them all the better for it.

Side by side with this development, however, and linked with it, we have seen a break-up of the old unified culture in which there was a commonly accepted overall view of things. We live in an era of the specialist, of the person who knows more and more about less and less. Although we have developed areas of densely cultivated knowledge, they just don't link up into any kind of network of ideas. The central split is of course between science and the humanities, but the fissures extend and proliferate within these 'two cultures' to produce a seriously fragmented system of knowledge.[2] This very modern problem of iso-lated specialization presents us with the acute difficulty of having to try to make sense of our knowledge piecemeal. It's as though we have just four or five pieces of a jigsaw puzzle and we can't make out what the whole picture is supposed to be.

There is, therefore, for anyone who is at all reflective, a pressing need – as much as there was for our primitive ancestors – to find the other bits of the jigsaw. There are, of course, many people willing to supply the missing pieces. The Roman Catholic Church, for example, is an ancient and venerable institution, and in the course of 2,000 years it has worked out all the answers. You only have to buy a copy of the latest catechism to find all the questions and all the answers neatly set out. Should any fresh questions arise, these will be swiftly answered by an encyclical from the Vatican. Many people find that this system deals with the mystery of life very satisfactorily. The same goes for Islam, which also lays down a conclusive and thoroughgoing context of mean-ing for human life. Marxism too, in its various forms, provided – at least until recently – a comparatively all-embracing world view that ex-plained everything in terms of economic evolution leading to a political and social utopia.

Those whom the more established systems of thought fail to satisfy can turn to any number of 'cults' or fringe religious groups, even psychological and political movements, for something that will validate their aspirations and make them feel positive and progressive. And it is possible to go from one to another, to change your direction, as often as you like. I knew an Englishwoman in India who claimed to have changed her religion seventeen times. She had started off as a Roman Catholic and had worked her way through the Vedanta and the Swedenborgian Church and the Ramakrishna Mission and many others. By the time I knew her, when she was middle-aged, she was a Seventh

Day Adventist, and even then thinking of moving on to something else, because this religion prohibited the consumption of tea. I remember visiting her once (this was in Kalimpong), and while we were having a nice cup of tea together there was a knock on the door and she turned pale. 'My God,' she whispered, 'That's the minister', and quickly hid the teapot. I believe she went on to Australia, but whether or not she found something that suited her better I don't know. One may laugh or one may cry at the sort of predicament she was in – but she was at least searching for the truth in her own way.

The fact is that, whether one is making a point of searching for the truth or not, it is simply not possible to avoid the practice of philosophy altogether. Everybody has a philosophy of some kind. It is just that some people are good at philosophizing and others are not. You can meet all sorts of people who have developed, without any academic training of any kind, an articulated philosophy of their own that is consistent and integrated. But whereas these individuals may have worked out a clear conceptualized version of their own attitude towards life as a whole, others may have only a very rudimentary or embryonic idea of what they take to be the central reality and purpose of life. Like it or not, we all begin as our remote ancestors did in a state of confusion and bewilderment, but it is up to us where we go from there.

It is as if you woke up one day to find yourself in a strange bed in some kind of inn. You don't know how you got there and you don't know where you are – except that it's somehow a temporary place to stay, with people coming and people going. All you know is that it's not your own place and you don't recognize the road it's on. You've just woken up and you're bewildered and confused and wondering what's going on. This is surely more or less how we feel about finding ourselves in the world at all. Here we are with a body, two eyes, two ears, a mouth, a nose, thoughts ... dropped off in the middle of England or wherever, dumped down in the tail-end of the twentieth century. What brought us here, we just don't know. We just wake up and here we are.

So when you wake up in this imaginary inn all you want to know is where you go from here. You need someone to give you a map showing the surrounding country, so that you can see the route you have come by so far and the direction you need to take to reach your destination. And this, as one might expect by now, is where Buddhism comes in. It is when the human condition is looked at in these quite elementary, even existential, terms that the teaching of the Buddha seems to come into its own.

Encountering Buddhism, what we discover, essentially, is a very comprehensive system of thought. (The word 'thought' is not ideal, but it must do for the time being.) This is not to say that the different forms of Buddhism that have arisen over more than 2,000 years all necessarily hang together neatly. But as well as being used as a blanket term covering the whole range of different approaches to the teaching, 'Buddhism' needs also to be appreciated in essential terms as representing a consistent and complete philosophical scheme.

Encountering Buddhism concretely, however, coming into contact with actual Buddhist groups, meeting flesh-and-blood Buddhist individuals, we find only too often the same sort of piecemeal approach that characterizes modern knowledge as a whole. There are a lot of schools in Buddhism (and they are 'schools' rather than 'sects') – Theravāda, Zen, Pure Land, T'ien-t'ai, Gelug, Kagyu, Nyingma, and so on. But it is rare to find followers of one school of Buddhism knowing anything much about the teachings of any other school. I have had a good deal of contact with Theravāda Buddhists, for example (admittedly, in most cases, a very long time ago), and my experience was that – whether they came from Sri Lanka, Burma, or Thailand – they knew absolutely nothing about Zen. In the vast majority of cases they had not even heard of it. Conversely, one can meet Zen monks – even Zen masters – who haven't a clue about what the Theravāda might be. As the world becomes a smaller place this is gradually changing, but one has to be careful when picking up a book on Buddhism, or listening to someone talk about Buddhism, that one isn't just getting the version of Buddhism put forward by one particular school.

Within Buddhism there is also a tendency to present a partial and unbalanced account of the teaching. A particular set of doctrines may be set out very clearly, but they are not related to other doctrines that perhaps look at the same issue from a different angle. For instance, there is the teaching of *duḥkha*, that human existence is inherently unsatisfactory, that it can never be quite as we would like, that, indeed, even if we got everything we wanted, life would still be unsatisfactory. It is a fundamental doctrine, without which the whole of Buddhism rather loses its point. However, if it is not always firmly located within the context of the Four Noble Truths which go on to summarize the way to transcend it, the teaching of *duḥkha* will seem just a rather sour fact of life.

Take another doctrine, that of the *tathāgata-garbha* – literally the 'womb of Enlightenment' – according to which all sentient existence carries within it the 'seed' of Buddhahood, of supreme and perfect

Enlightenment. If this doctrine of universal potential Buddhahood is not related to the Noble Eightfold Path which adumbrates the necessary steps to be taken in order to realize Enlightenment, we can come away with the notion that we actually have Buddhahood in the palm of our hand, as it were, and that all we have to do is wake up to the fact. Such teachings, if not put in their proper context and related to an overall framework, can be quite misleading.

This goes for meditation too. We can no doubt very usefully take up meditation as a purely psychological exercise. But as soon as we begin to see it as more than just a 'profane' training, as soon as we begin to acknowledge that it is some sort of 'sacred' or spiritual practice, we need to acquire some understanding of the general spiritual framework or context within which its practical spiritual purpose is defined. In the East it doesn't matter so much, because there the whole culture, the whole society, provides that framework, and if one has close personal contact with a good teacher then one doesn't need to know very much about the doctrine intellectually. But that situation does not obtain in the West, and if we are to take up Buddhist meditation we must have some knowledge of the general principles of Buddhism.

Buddhism is a vast subject. Therefore, putting it in a context which is familiar to the modern Western mind is not to be taken too literally – it is not like finding a big box into which we can fit a smaller box. It is a matter rather of laying out the Buddhist system of thought as a whole in terms that should be sufficiently familiar to all of us – as a way of looking at the world – not to require much explanation. And the idea that functions most comprehensively in this way is the principle of evolution, derived from the biological sciences. The fact that the Christian faith in particular has become reconciled to this principle only with the greatest difficulty makes it also a useful tool in highlighting some of the more distinctive features of the Buddhist vision. Nothing like the kind of *tour de force* we meet with in the works of the Catholic thinker Teilhard de Chardin is required to bring Buddhism and modern evolutionary ideas together.

We now know that the theory of evolution was anticipated by a number of thinkers, by Kant, Hegel, and others – and even, according to some, by Aristotle himself. But Darwin was the first to trace the operation of evolution in detail within the field of biology. To attempt to refute the principle of evolution in that field today would be like saying the earth is flat. It is the given basis for all the biological sciences. If anything, the idea has invaded all sorts of other disciplines, from politics to astronomy, so that one could fairly say that just as the Elizabethan age was dominated by the concepts of order and hierarchy, so the modern world is dominated by the concept of evolution.

In taking up an idea that is generally understood in scientific or at least academic applications and applying it in a spiritual context, we have, of course, to draw some precise boundaries. Scientific knowledge depends on the evidence of the senses – but, just because Buddhism has never tried to resist the evidence of the senses, that does not make it a 'scientific religion'. It is certainly true that Buddhism's appeal in the West owes much to the spirit of empirical, open-minded inquiry which the Buddha laid down as axiomatic to the spiritual quest – and this lack of dogmatism does align Buddhism in some important respects with the Greek scientific spirit rather than with the dominant religious traditions in the modern West. Equally axiomatic to the Buddhist notion of the spiritual quest, however, is the recognition of a transcendental Reality – which is not, of course, a provable scientific hypothesis. As a practising Buddhist one starts from the evidence of one's own experience, which will tend to support more and more the idea of a spiritual order of evolution, and it is on the basis of this evidence that biological evolution carries conviction – not the other way round. Therefore, if we look at ourselves as in any way constituting some kind of key to the universe, then on the basis of our own experience of progression we may fairly conclude that progression is in some way inherent in the universe.

In this respect, at least, Buddhism inclines more towards a traditional, pre-scientific viewpoint. If we look at a traditional civilization, we find that everything, every activity, every piece of knowledge, is linked in with ideas of a metaphysical order. Ordinary things, ordinary events, accepted ideas, are not just of practical use. They have a symbolic value, they point beyond themselves, they have meaning. Amidst our own fragmented, 'specialist', economically defined culture we may find it difficult to appreciate this attitude, but it is the basis for the Tantra, and it was the world view of our own society until comparatively recently. According to this view everything is interconnected and nothing can ever really be ordinary – in the sense of being without a deeper meaning – at all. Rather than look for scientific proof of spiritual realities, we may say, paraphrasing G.K. Chesterton, that it is because we no longer believe in the gods that we no longer believe in ourselves. Our project as Buddhists must be to replace a mechanistic universe with one that has meaning, that carries throughout its fabric intimations of spiritual values.

Buddhism therefore looks at the rational knowledge derived from the senses in the light of a knowledge that is derived not from the senses and reason alone, but from a fusion of reason with emotion in a higher faculty of archetypal knowledge which we may call 'vision', 'insight', or 'imagination'. It is not a question of justifying Buddhism in scientific terms, but rather of understanding sense-derived knowledge by means of knowledge that is not sense-based. In other words, the knowledge that is derived from the senses fits into a much larger pattern of knowledge that is not derived from the senses. From a Buddhist point of view, there is a hierarchy of levels of being and consciousness, a hierarchy of degrees of spiritual attainment, which seems to be reflected in, or as it were anticipated by, the whole process of biological evolution. It seems to make sense, therefore, to regard both biological evolution and the hierarchies of spiritual development as being – from the Buddhist point of view – in their separate spheres, exemplifications of a single law or principle.

It is clear that according to the principle of evolution life is not just existence. It is a process – a process of becoming – and humankind is not something apart from the rest of nature, as the theistic religions usually teach. Humankind itself also comes under the operation of this great process of becoming. It too is evolving and developing, not just towards new forms of existence and organization, but towards new and higher levels of being.

There are two different ways of looking at any evolving phenomenon: in terms of its past or in terms of its future; in terms of what it was or in terms of what it may come to be. The first of these ways of looking at phenomena – in terms of its origins – is traditionally called the genetic approach; the second – in terms of its destination or purpose – is the teleological method. So if we take an example of humankind at its best – someone who is intelligent, self-aware, morally responsible, sensitive to others and to the world around them – we should be able to look at them from each of these two perspectives. From a genetic perspective, we can look back at the complex evolutionary process described by Darwin, including that critical point at which self-consciousness – or more precisely, reflexive consciousness, which is roughly identifiable with specifically human consciousness – emerges from simple animal sense-consciousness. This whole process we can characterize, from the Buddhist point of view, as the 'lower evolution'. But there is also the teleological perspective: we can also look at what an aware human being may develop into, what they are in process of developing into, and this development we may distinguish as the 'higher evolution'. We have got so far in evolutionary terms propelled by the unconscious urge to grow and develop which fuels the origin of species, but to enter into the higher evolution takes conscious effort, or what we call spiritual practice. The lower evolution is the province of the biological sciences, leaving the higher evolution to be mapped out by the religions of the world, especially, of course, by Buddhism.

This sort of model of Buddhism is crucial to an understanding of who the Buddha is and what our own relationship to him might be. By means of it we can locate our own situation, which is probably a little short of our central figure of the fully integrated human being, and thus somewhere in the upper reaches of the lower evolution. We can also see the evolutionary process stretching ahead of us as far as Buddha-hood – and beyond, inasmuch as Buddhahood is not a terminal point, but is by its very 'nature' limitless. And somewhere in the midst of this continuum we can envisage another critical point, where Insight into the nature of Reality – Insight with a capital I – replaces our faint, confused, and intermittent apprehensions of something that transcends our common perception of things. In this way, we know where we stand, we know the direction we must take, and we have something to aim for.

Before focusing on those stages in the evolutionary process that concern us as individual human beings we can restate what has been said so far in traditional Buddhist terminology. According to Buddhism the nature of existence consists in change or 'becoming'. It is not simply some 'thing' that is subject to change – existence itself is change. And the specific manner of that change was expressed by the Buddha in a formula known in Sanskrit as *pratītya-samutpāda* and translated as 'conditioned co-production' or 'dependent origination'. This formula or law goes as follows: 'This being, that becomes; from the arising of this, that arises. This not being, that does not become; from the ceasing of this, that ceases.' So if existence is change, change is conditionality. Existence is seen as an infinitely complex and shifting pattern of physical and mental phenomena, all coming into being in dependence on certain conditions, and disappearing when those conditions disappear.

Pratītya-samutpāda is not traditionally invoked as a cosmological principle, but there is no reason why it should not be. In the *Dīgha Nikāya* of the Pali canon there is a very long discourse delivered by the Buddha, the *Aggañña Sutta*, which deals with the evolution of the universe and the origin of humankind. But for our present purposes we may say simply that in dependence upon the lower evolution arises the higher evolution.

What this does not mean is that the higher evolution is entirely the product of the lower evolution. *Pratītya-samutpāda* expresses the middle way between seeing the lower evolution as essentially the same process as the higher evolution and seeing them as completely different processes. The basic Buddhist approach is in this sense scientific – it describes what happens without necessarily committing itself to an interpretation of those facts.

Within this universal framework of conditionality, however, there are two types of conditionality. On the one hand there is a 'cyclic' mode of conditionality, a process of reaction between opposite factors: death arising in dependence on birth, good in dependence on evil, happiness in dependence on suffering – and vice versa. It is a characteristic of human experience that is all too familiar – as Keats puts it: 'Ay, in the very temple of delight / Veil'd melancholy has her sovran shrine'.[3] This is saṃsāra or the round of existence, as depicted in the Tibetan version of the Wheel of Life.

On the other hand there is a cumulative development of positive factors progressively augmenting each other, and this 'spiral' mode of conditionality provides the basis for the spiritual life. Thus in dependence on the arising of faith, joy arises, and so on in an ascending series of mental states all the way up to Enlightenment itself. The essential characteristic of a positive mental state is that it does not produce a negative reaction but instead produces a further positive factor. An act of true generosity, for example, is not succeeded by a niggling resentment when your gift does not seem to be appreciated. You simply derive joy from giving. It hardly needs saying that the cyclical principle governs the lower evolution, while the spiral mode of conditionality comprises the higher evolution.

The Buddha's working out, in his first discourse after his Enlightenment, of the principle of *pratītya-samutpāda* as the Four Noble Truths can be correlated with the evolution model equally simply. The first and second Noble Truths, which are that pain is inherent in sentient existence and that this pain arises in dependence – ultimately – upon craving, are concerned with the lower evolution. The third and fourth Noble Truths, which are, respectively, that this pain ceases with the ceasing of craving, and that the way to bring about an end to craving is by undertaking the Noble Eightfold Path, take us into the higher evolution.

By taking an evolutionary perspective we can discern some absolutely fundamental practical principles of the spiritual life. Within the lower evolution forms of life develop as a group – evolution works as a collective process – whereas the higher evolution is necessarily individual, which means that one individual can outstrip the rest. It is for this reason that self-awareness, mindfulness, is the starting point – the growing point – of the higher evolution. It is as though self-awareness generates a degree of energy sufficient to carry you through the whole process of the higher evolution in a single lifetime. Buddhist practice is concerned solely and exclusively with the development of the individual, that is, with the higher evolution. Once this is clear we can bring the whole range of Buddhist teachings into focus.

The Buddha lays down a path of practice leading to Enlightenment, but then he says very emphatically, 'You must walk the path yourselves. I've walked it for myself, but I can't walk it for you. No one can save another. No one can purify another. It's up to you to do it for yourselves.' In this sense Buddhism is a do-it-yourself religion. The corollary of this is that anyone who makes the effort can obtain the same results. There aren't some chosen few who can do it and others who can't. If no one is going to do it for you, this also means that if you make the effort, you can attain. You don't even have to call yourself a Buddhist. If you accept the principles and follow the path, you will infallibly get the right results.

This is one reason why Buddhism is, by its very nature, a tolerant religion. Buddhists are not tolerant out of sheer indifference or apathy. They are tolerant because everybody has to find out the Truth for themselves. This is the nature of the Buddhist path. You have to allow others the same freedom that you claim for yourself – freedom to grow, to develop spiritually, in their own way. Therefore there is no conception of religious war or religious persecution in Buddhism. You find, for example, that the king of Thailand, who is the Buddhist king of a largely but not wholly Buddhist country, has as one of his titles 'Protector of all Religions'.

So there is no compulsion. The Buddha's teaching, the Dharma, is called, in Pali – the ancient language in which much of it was first written down – *ehipassiko dhamma*, that is, 'the teaching (*dhamma*) of come (*ehi*) and see (*passiko*)'. It is the teaching that says come and see for yourself. Don't accept just on trust. Believe because you understand, experience and verify for yourself. Don't believe just because the Buddha tells you. This is what the Buddha himself said: 'Monks, don't accept what I say just out of respect for me. Just as gold is tested in the fire, so test my words in the fire of spiritual experience.'

When the Buddha's aunt and foster-mother, Mahāprajāpati Gautami, confused by the conflicting versions of his teaching given even in his own lifetime by his disciples, asked him straight, 'What do you really teach?' the Buddha replied that she could work it out for herself: 'Whatever teachings you can be sure conduce to tranquillity and not to greed and hatred; to freedom and not to enslavement; to decrease of worldly ties and not to increase of them; to contentment and not to covetousness; to solitude and not to social distractions; to energy and not to sluggishness; to delight in good and not to delight in evil; of these teachings you can be sure that they constitute my Dharma.'[4]

One of the most prevalent ways in which some Buddhists take a one-sided view of the Dharma is in thinking of it in an exclusively negative manner, as just a matter of rooting out the whole of the lower evolution and leaving it at that. But it is evident from passages like those quoted above that the Buddha's own conception of it was one of positive growth, of a conscious effort to evolve and progress as an individual. As well as leaving the lower evolution behind, we need also to take some positive steps in the direction of the higher evolution. As well as giving up meanness we want to cultivate generosity. As well as avoiding being harsh and callous we want to develop kindness. And there is a set of four meditation practices which are specifically concerned with developing the whole range of positive emotion. These meditations are called the four *brahma vihāras*, 'the abodes of the gods'. The first consists in the development of *mettā* or love towards all living beings – a desire for the well-being of others, a wish that they may grow and develop. The second *brahma vihāra* is *karuṇā* or compassion for those who are stuck, whose growth is stunted. Thirdly there is *muditā* or 'sympathetic joy' in the happiness of others – which is like when you go out into the garden in early summer and see the flowers all springing up and blooming. And the fourth is *upekṣā*, equanimity or peace, an experience not of sitting back and putting your feet up, but of a vibrant spiritual equilibrium.

The four *brahma vihāras* do not come naturally; they are not endowments of the lower evolution. They have to be consciously developed, for, as we have seen, spiritual development is the development of consciousness. Whereas the lower evolution is an unconscious development on the material level, the higher evolution is a conscious development on the mental level. At the same time the whole of evolution, lower and higher, is a continuous process. Of the two general scientific theories of evolution, that it is a mechanistic, random process, and the opposite view, that it could not have taken place without some kind of purpose or direction, the Buddhist approach would go with the second view. It is very broadly 'vitalist' in that it recognizes a will to Enlightenment somehow present in all forms of life and manifesting in any gesture of consideration or act of intelligent good will. With the beginning of the evolutionary process you get the impression of a sort of fumbling, with a lot of false starts – it seems a bit hit-or-miss. But then as you follow it further, whatever it is that stands behind the evolutionary process seems to become surer of itself, as it were, and to define itself more clearly as time goes by. And with the emergence of the aware individual human being undertaking the spiritual path it becomes fully conscious of itself, thereby speeding up the whole process.

The Buddhist has to tread very lightly in this area to avoid misunderstanding. Evolution is just a metaphor or model for Buddhism, a temporal model. In speaking of some 'thing', some reality *behind* the evolutionary process, we are simply using a different model, a spatial model. If we speak in terms of developing from one stage to another, that is to look at reality in temporal terms. But if we speak of what is there all the time, the absolute reality which is always here and now, that is to speak in spatial terms. So this is the function of the 'Will to Enlightenment' or *bodhicitta*, in this context – to transcend these spatio-temporal models. It is not a sort of cosmic life principle – not the life-force of the universe, or any kind of causative first principle – but rather a liberation principle, a will to transcend the universe or saṁsāra.

We may say, in fact, that transcendence, self-transcendence, is what the whole of evolution, from the amoeba upwards, is about. We can say further that this evolutionary principle of self-transcendence is expressed in its highest and most fully self-conscious form in the figure of the Bodhisattva, the one who, according to Mahāyāna Buddhism, dedicates himself or herself to the cause of helping all sentient existence to Enlightenment. The Will to Enlightenment of a Bodhisattva is a fully committed volition to perpetual self-transcendence. And from the Bodhisattva to the Buddha there is only, as it were, a step.

It is from this perspective, seeing spiritual development in terms of perpetual self-transcendence, that we can best appreciate the often half-understood Buddhist concept of *anātman*, or 'no-self'. This is sometimes interpreted as meaning that we don't really exist, that there's a sort of hole where one imagines one's self to be. In fact, the point of this teaching is that we have no substantial unchanging self, no soul. Indeed, putting it more dynamically and experientially, we can say that for radical change, radical development, to take place – for a fully conscious self-transcendence to be possible – there *can* be no unchanging self.

We may look at Buddhism from a purely academic perspective as just an activity or philosophical position of a number of individuals calling themselves Buddhists. On the other hand, we can take the vast and awe-inspiring perspective of the Buddha's teaching itself. From this latter perspective, we are all frail, impermanent beings, born into the world and passing out of it with apparently little to show for our trouble – but at the same time we embody the universal possibility of Enlightenment. Just as the scientific concept of evolution involves a progression towards new biological organisms through periods of time that are practically unimaginable, so, according to Buddhism, our own lives take their place in a context of literally unimaginable temporal duration, in which, however, they are of literally cosmic importance. For among all the life-forms in the universe, from the amoeba to the highest realms of the gods, it is only the kind of sentient life to which human beings conform that can be, in the words of Lama Govinda, 'the vehicle for the rediscovery of the transcendental and inconceivable nature of mind or consciousness' – that can become, in short, a Buddha.

2

The Way to Enlightenment

All human beings are capable of evolving into Buddhas, but one man alone opened the way for the rest of humanity to follow. To be strictly accurate, we should say 're-opened', because traditionally speaking there had been other Buddhas, many other pioneers on the path of the higher evolution, before him. But when we speak of *the* Buddha we refer to Siddhārtha Gautama, who discovered the path on the full-moon day of the lunar month of April/May, in the year 542BCE. The way he himself put it was this: 'Suppose a man wandering in a forest wilderness found an ancient path, an ancient trail, travelled by men of old, and he followed it, and by doing so he discovered an ancient city, an ancient royal capital, where men of old had lived, with parks and groves and lakes, walled round and beautiful to see. In such wise have I found the ancient path, the ancient trail, travelled by the Fully Enlightened Ones of old.'[5]

Hence the very special place in the Buddhist calendar of Vaiśākha Purnima, the full-moon day of the Indian month Vaiśākha. Vaiśākha in Pali is Vesakha, and this translates into Sinhalese as Wesak, which gives its name to the most important of Buddhist festivals. At Wesak Buddhists celebrate what they regard as being the greatest event on record, the occasion when, for the first time in recorded history, an unenlightened being, a man, became an Enlightened being, an Enlightened man. They commemorate the day when Siddhārtha Gautama finally freed himself from all human conditionings, all human limitations, to become as it were one with Reality, to become even, we may say, a living embodiment of the Truth, a Buddha.

It might seem surprising, therefore, that there should be a certain amount of confusion as to what is really being celebrated at Wesak. However, whenever I used to be invited to take part in a Wesak celebration in India, whether as a speaker or in some other capacity, what I used to be asked to do was to honour (or grace) with my presence – such is the Indian style of courtesy in such matters – 'the Thrice Sacred Day (or Festival)'. So why 'thrice sacred'? Surely once is enough? Either something is sacred or it isn't – so you might think. But of course there is a reason for this designation. According to some sources the Vaiśākha Purnima is the anniversary of not one but three events: the Buddha's birth, his attainment of Enlightenment, and also his final passing away or parinirvāṇa. They are all supposed to have taken place on the same day – in different years of course, but by quite a coincidence on the same full-moon day. It must be said, however, that this tradition of a thrice-sacred Vaiśākha Purnima rests on a very late tradition originating in Sri Lanka and thence spreading to other Theravāda countries. The rest of the Buddhist world, the Mahāyāna Buddhist countries, celebrate the Buddha's birth and his parinirvāṇa on other days of the year, and this does seem to have been the earlier – and also the more reasonable – arrangement.

As well as having different ideas about whether or not Wesak marks anything besides the Buddha's Enlightenment, Buddhists in different parts of the world have different national traditions in the way they go about marking it. In Sri Lanka and Burma you will find people lighting candles and offering them in homage to the Buddha's memory. In Tibet it will be butter lamps, and it will be a particular number of butter lamps – 108 or 1,008 of them. In many Buddhist countries you will hear people chanting verses in praise of the Buddha, sometimes for hours on end, even all day and all night. In other places there will be lectures and discussions, and some people of course will simply be meditating. On a more social level you will find monks being fed – in some Buddhist countries this is a very popular pastime on any festive occasion. You gather together as many monks as possible, line them up in rows on the floor and give them food. Monks are traditionally supposed to have very healthy appetites and in some Buddhist quarters the amount of merit you get from feeding a monk is said to be directly linked to the amount of your food the monk eats. In these circumstances, therefore, hospitality is not stinted, and certainly not refused. Buddhists in the West follow the lead given by these older traditions, of course, but many of them are in the process of developing their own cultural tradition of celebrating Wesak.

At whatever level and in whatever fashion Buddhists celebrate Wesak they are unified by its one central theme and purpose, which is to rejoice at the emergence of a Buddha in the world. In this they are following a tradition which goes back a very long way indeed, and we have only to look among the earliest examples of Indian Buddhist stone carvings to find evidence of this. A particularly striking composition places the Buddha, in symbolic form, on a throne, surrounded by monks, nuns, and lay-people all with their hands joined together above their heads and all making offerings of garlands, fruits, scarves – all sorts of offerings being made in all sorts of ways. What is really notable about this scene is the expression of absolute joy that all these figures wear, and the joyful way they worship and make offerings to the Buddha. The impression one gets is that an event of overwhelming, cosmic importance must have taken place to be celebrated in this exultant and really spectacular manner. It would hardly be an exaggeration to say that the artist has made these worshippers look positively mad with joy – if one can think of Buddhists really being mad about anything. But that seems to be what they are – mad with joy.

Such is the only emotional response – as this artist proposes, at least – that can do justice to the Buddha's realization of the ultimate possibility of human development. Yet the deep roots of the joy expressed by his followers at Wesak lie not just in the fact that he attained Enlightenment for himself, as it were. They lie in the fact that he opened the way, he blazed the trail, for others to follow after him. The question of how the Buddha became Enlightened is therefore not just theoretical. Of course, you can approach it theoretically if you wish, as you can approach any question theoretically, but essentially it is a question of the greatest practical importance. The Buddha did not inherit Enlightenment, he was not born to be Enlightened. He attained Enlightenment only after many years of struggle – and even after making mistakes. Through his own efforts in his own life he showed how we too by our own efforts can gain Enlightenment.

This provides, in fact, a whole extra line of approach to the Dharma, the Way to Enlightenment. You can, as already suggested, think of it in terms of evolution, of progressive stages to be followed like a sort of road, with so many milestones along it marking the distance you've travelled. And so you have the three great stages of the path – ethics, meditation, and wisdom – as well as many other ways of subdividing and classifying the Way to Enlightenment. But you can also approach it from a more unusual angle – that is, in terms of the events of the Buddha's life.

To contemplate the biographical details of the Buddha's early life is to be concerned not just with the spiritual path followed by a man who lived 2,500 years ago. It is to contemplate a path which one can follow here and now, a path that one is committed to following if one is a Buddhist, if one has Buddhahood as one's ultimate goal. In other words, when as Buddhists we celebrate the Buddha's Enlightenment, we are not just rejoicing in a thing of the past. We are reminding ourselves that it is high time we started to think of our own Enlightenment, if indeed we have not already done so – and if we have, to think of it more persistently, more seriously, and more deeply.

We shall therefore run through the salient events of the Buddha's early life, to get a general idea of the way to Enlightenment, and then take up for more detailed examination certain crucial episodes or features of his biography that have a definite bearing on our own process of development towards Enlightenment. Like the story of the Buddha's life as a whole, these particularly notable elements are in substance historical, inasmuch as we know they actually did happen. However, the versions that have come down to us contain a certain amount of legendary material, and it is this legendary material that helps to bring out the universal significance, the inner spiritual dimension, of the external events. The mythical aspect makes it clear, among other things, that these events are concerned not with one man's spiritual career, but with the career of every man and woman who aspires to grow and develop as an individual.

It is very often said that Siddhārtha Gautama, who became the Buddha, was born in India, and a hundred years ago this would have been true. But owing to changing political boundaries we would have to say today that his birth took place in the southern part of what is now Nepal. He was born into a tribe called the Śākyans, who had inhabited that particular area in the foothills of the Himalayas for many centuries. Nor is it quite true – as it is, again, often said – that his father, Suddhodana Gautama, was the king of the tribe. He did certainly hold the title of rajah at the time of Siddhārtha's birth, but today he would probably be called a president. Like other small tribes in north-eastern India at that time, the Śākyans had a semi-republican form of government, with a leader elected from the clan assembly for a fixed period of twelve years. Towards the end of the Buddha's lifetime the little republics of India were swallowed up by the developing Magadha empire, but at the time of his birth they were, for the most part, in a flourishing condition.

Siddhārtha's mother, Māyādevī, was the daughter of the chief of a neighbouring tribe, the Koliyas. It was then the custom, as it still is the custom in many parts of India, for the first child to be born in the house of the mother's parents. When she felt her time approaching, therefore, Māyādevī set off from Kapilavastu, the Śākyan capital, to make for her father's city, carried, as far as we know, in a palanquin. She was still only halfway there when, seized with the pangs of labour, she dismounted, and in a grove of sāl trees at a little place called Lumbinī gave birth to the future Buddha. She died shortly afterwards – seven days later, according to tradition.

Siddhārtha was reared by his maternal aunt, Mahāprājapati Gautami, whom his father had also married. There is really little more to be said about his childhood – it took place, after all, 2,500 years ago. A single authentic incident stands out from it, one that took place when he was five, six, or perhaps seven years old, on the occasion of the annual ploughing ceremony. In primarily agricultural civilizations all over the world, the sowing of the first seed in the spring was a matter of magical and mythical significance, and the first ploughing was always undertaken by the king or chief. It was one of the duties of the old emperors of China, and until quite recently the emperor of Japan used to inaugurate the ploughing every year, so obviously this was one of the jobs that fell to Siddhārtha's father to carry out. Later accounts tell us that it was done with a golden plough drawn by beautiful white oxen (storytellers love to embroider their material). But leaving aside the precise quality of the equipment used, what we can say with confidence is that Siddhārtha's father performed this ceremony and that Siddhārtha was brought along to watch.

The little boy was put on one side on a little bank in the shade of a jambu or rose-apple tree, and it was there that he had what we would describe nowadays as a spontaneous mystical experience. According to the Buddha himself, as he reminisced to his disciples a great many years later, what he experienced beneath the rose-apple tree was a sort of superconscious state known as *dhyāna*. So deep was his absorption that he never saw the ploughing at all, and he had still not emerged from the experience when they came to take him home.

It is at this point that an interesting legendary anecdote finds its way into the episode. The legend has it that although it was noon when the ploughing started, and evening by the time the ceremony was all over, the shadow of the rose-apple tree had not moved during that time. On a literal level this would be what we call a miracle, but it is perhaps more meaningful if we take it symbolically. The obvious implication is that the sun stood still; and the implication on the symbolic level is that for the young Siddhārtha time itself had stopped.

Later on, as we shall see, this experience – or rather the memory of this experience – was to have a crucial bearing on the direction of Siddhārtha's spiritual career. But meanwhile, mystical experience or no mystical experience, he was a Kṣatriya, a warrior, and he would have been brought up like one. That was his caste – the caste of the whole tribe. It was a Kṣatriya tribe, and so he was literally born a warrior, as others were born Brahmins (priests), Vaiṣyas (traders and farmers), or Śūdras (labourers) – just as they are today, although these four castes are now subdivided into some 2,000 subcastes.

The future Buddha spent his formative years not in the close study of philosophy and in religious practices, but in the tilt-yard, acquiring the arts of archery and spear-throwing, swordplay, and the skilful handling of a war-chariot. With his patrician background he would have received the best martial training available. He would also have been initiated into the various traditions, customs, beliefs, and superstitions of the tribe, and he would have learned a little history and genealogy too. Of course, whatever he learned would have been by word of mouth from the elders of the tribe. It is not in fact clear whether the Buddha ever learned to read or write. We must imagine him as a man who was cultured, educated, and well-bred without ever having attended any-thing like a school (it is, in any case, questionable whether education has really anything to do with going to school). He led on the whole a quite comfortable, well-to-do life, had no particular responsibilities, and was doted on by his father.

Siddhārtha's upbringing was not, however, quite so simple and straightforward as all that. Shortly after his birth, his father had taken him to a *rishi*, the sage Asita, to have his horoscope cast. This was common practice, as it still is in India today. There is hardly anybody, even among the Westernized so-called élite, who does not have this done for their children – especially for their sons. You want to know what is going to happen to your child, what sort of a career he or she will have, so you go to an astrologer. It is not known exactly how Siddhārtha's horoscope was cast, but we know that he was placed in the arms of Asita, and that the *rishi* made his calculations. He predicted that the child would have a remarkable future: Siddhārtha would either become a great Kṣatriya, a great warrior and ruler, or else he would give it all up and become a great spiritual master.

Suddhodana was deeply disturbed at this prognostication, of course. He liked the idea of his son becoming an illustrious conqueror – he liked it very much – but he was appalled at the idea that the lad might take it into his head to retire from the world altogether and devote his talents to the spiritual quest. The older Siddhārtha grew, the more Suddhodana turned the matter over in his mind. He thought, 'I want him to grow up like me. I want him to be brave and strong and extend the territory of the tribe, and – if the *rishi* is right – to become a great ruler and maybe conquer all of India. He must not be allowed to waste his time over all this religious nonsense. Therefore he must be prevented from thinking too deeply about anything; he must not be introduced to the more unpalatable facts of life – at least not too early. His heart must be set firmly on worldly things.'

So Suddhodana was determined that the young prince should want for nothing, that all he should learn about life should be how to enjoy it to the most refined pitch of sensual pleasure. The Buddha later related in one of his autobiographical discourses how his father had provided him with three beautiful mansions, one for each season, so that he should never feel discomfort from the heat or the cold or the rains. And he recounted also how these mansions were filled with alluring dancing girls and bewitching singing girls, and how his days and nights were spent in drinking, dancing, and singing, one pleasure succeeding another, with hardly a moment for sadness.

At sixteen he was married off to a cousin, Yaśodharā. It was an arranged marriage, of course, just as in India today a marriage is nearly always negotiated by the families of the bride and bridegroom rather than by the young people themselves. He settled down happily enough and in this way for many years his life went on. All the same, though, he seems to have had an underlying sense of dissatisfaction with the life he was leading. He chafed at the bit. When the news was brought to him that his wife had given birth to a son his reaction was not the usual one of a proud father. Asked what the boy should be called, he said, 'A fetter has been born to me. Call him Rāhula,'[6] for this is what the name Rāhula means – 'fetter'. It was as if he sensed what his father had been trying to do all his life. Somehow he knew that Suddhodana was trying to bind him down: bind him down with pleasure, bind him down with property, bind him down with power, with family, with wife and child. He knew what was happening. He neglected his martial exercises and lost interest in the amusements and distractions laid on for him indoors. Domestic life held no joy for him.

Increasingly he took himself off for long periods in order to think, and at some point he evidently had some sort of spiritual crisis – though this is not of course how the early scriptures put it. This psychological and spiritual turning point is known among Buddhists everywhere in the form of a dramatic narrative called the Four Sights. Whether this is a legend, whether it is an external projection of an experience arising out of intense inner questioning, or whether it actually happened in something like the way the story has come down to us, it is impossible for us to say for sure. What is certain is that the Four Sights crystallize in a very powerful form some of the fundamental teachings of Buddhism, as well as throwing light on the Buddha's own early spiritual development.

The story goes that one bright morning Siddhārtha called his charioteer to harness the horses for an outing. 'Let's see what is going on in the world, see what people are up to,' he said. The charioteer shook his head. 'I'm afraid we can't do that – it's more than my job's worth. You know the king has said you are not to go out among the people.' But the young prince insisted: 'Don't worry. I'll take full responsibility. If the king has anything to say about it, let him say it to me. But let's go.' So the horses were whipped up and away they went. They drove out into the village and Siddhārtha saw life going on much as he might have expected – until his attention was arrested by the sight of a very old man.

The traditional accounts give a graphic description of this old man's appearance – feeble, withered, and bent over, his bones sticking out, tottering along on a stick. He had a long white beard and the rheum was trickling from his eyes. If this seems to be laying it on a bit thick, it would not seem so in India. There, old people, even today – because of the climate and the hard life – can look very old indeed. At no more than fifty or sixty they can look about a hundred years old. We have to remember that according to the legend his father had deliberately secluded him from anything unpleasant about life, and this included old age. So when Siddhārtha saw this very old man, he pointed at him and said, 'Who ... what ... is that?'

The charioteer thought, 'Well, he'll have to find out sooner or later,' and he said, 'It's an old man.' 'But why is he like that? Why is he so bent? Why do all his bones stick out? Why is that fluid trickling out from his eyes?' The charioteer was not used to fielding this sort of question, except perhaps from children. He said simply, 'Well, he's just an old man.' Obviously Siddhārtha was not satisfied by this: 'But how has he got like that?' 'It just happens,' the charioteer explained gently. 'You don't have to do anything to get old – you just get old. It's natural, I'm afraid – everybody gets old.' The young prince felt his flesh creep. 'What, everybody?' he asked, and the charioteer said, 'Well, yes, of course. Everybody.' 'What about me? Will I become like that?' The charioteer nodded: 'The king, your father, the queen, your mother, your wife, myself, and you too – all of us – are subject to old age.'

We are told that Siddhārtha received this intelligence like an elephant struck by a thunderbolt, and he broke into a cold sweat with the shock. 'What is the use of being young?' he lamented. 'What is the use of this vitality and strength, if it all ends in such emaciation and frailty?' He was sick at heart. 'That's enough for today, I think. Let's go home,' he said, and as they rattled back to the palace he brooded over the knowledge he had been given.

This, then, is the legend of the first Sight. Siddhārtha may or may not have literally clapped eyes on an old man for the first time in this way, but there is no mistaking the real significance of it. He might have seen, perhaps, many old men before, but somehow missed really seeing them. That day, perhaps, he saw an old man *as though* for the first time. This is the way it goes, of course. We see a thing – we see it maybe every day of our lives, just as we see the sun rising and the sun setting – but we don't really see it because we are not aware and we don't think. We see but we don't see. We are blind. One might work in an old people's home for years without taking in the fact of old age to any great depth. Then when we develop some awareness, some clarity, we can find that things appear to us in such a fresh light that it is as if we never saw them before. So Siddhārtha realized, truly realized for the first time in his life, that there was such a thing as old age, and that youth would be brief, even for him.

Shaken as he was by this realization, Siddhārtha went out again a few days later – so the legend has it – and again he saw something he had never seen before. What he saw was a sick man, lying by the roadside with an attack of fever or something of that sort, tossing this way and that, with no one to care for him. Again Siddhārtha asked the charioteer to explain to him what was going on: 'Tell me what has happened to this man. What is wrong with him? Why is he lying there beside the road? Why is he twitching? Why is he shaking and shivering? Why are his eyes rolling so wildly? Why does his face look so ghastly?' Of course the charioteer had to tell him, 'Well, he's ill.' And Siddhārtha, who had apparently enjoyed blooming health up to that time, wanted to know whether he too would be likely to suffer in this way: 'Does this happen to other people? Will it happen to me?' So again the charioteer drove the point home: 'All men, all women, are liable to sickness. It might come at any time. At any moment strength and health may go from us and then we must suffer sickness.' So again Siddhārtha had something to ponder over as he returned to the palace.

But after a few days off they went once more in the chariot, and this time he saw four men coming towards them carrying something between them on a sort of stretcher, the poles of which were balanced on their shoulders. Lying on the stretcher there was a man wrapped in a yellow sheet. His face was exposed, but there was something odd about it. He didn't move a muscle. The face was quite expressionless, stiff-looking, and the eyes were closed.

Of course, you can still see this sight any day of the week in India. An Indian funeral is rather different from what most of us are used to in the West. Here, when you die you are smuggled away in a box, and that's that. You are just quietly disposed of like so much garbage that no one wants to look at. You're put into the incinerator or into a little hole in the ground and covered over. But in India it isn't like that. In India you are laid out in the best room of the house and all your friends and relations come round to have a good look and say, 'Ah, it looks just like him. It's old so-and-so to the life. Well, he looks quite happy, quite peaceful. Yes, goodbye then, old fellow.' They shed a tear and throw a few flowers on the corpse, and then it is hoisted on the shoulders of four strong men and borne through the streets with the face still uncovered. So the corpse is jolting along, crowds of people following behind in the heat, and the people passing by look and say, 'Oh yes, there's old so-and-so – didn't know he had died.'

This sort of procession is what Siddhārtha saw, and he said to the charioteer, 'That's very strange. Why are they carrying that man like that? What are they doing? What's he done?' The charioteer replied in his usual laconic style, 'Well, this is a dead body.' We have to remember, of course, that death was one of those matters Siddhārtha was supposed to have been kept in the dark about, so he was mystified by this explanation. 'Dead? What do you mean dead?' And the charioteer again had to expatiate a little: 'Well, you can see, he's stiff, lifeless, doesn't breathe, doesn't see, doesn't hear, he doesn't feel. He's dead. They are taking him to the burning ground. They are going to burn the body. It's what happens at death.' Siddhārtha gasped with horror: 'Does this too happen to everybody? Will everybody come to this, this death, as you call it? Will I too come to death?' The charioteer drew a long sigh. 'Yes. Your father, your mother, your wife, your child – they must all die one day. I must die. You must die. Everybody who is born must die. There have been millions of men and women born since the world began and every single one of them has died. No doubt there will be millions more born in the future, but every single one of them will die. No one can ever escape the cold hand of death. Death is king of all.' So, more sad, more thoughtful, more anguished than ever, Siddhārtha ordered the charioteer to turn round and head back to the palace.

Over these three outings with his charioteer he had come up against what nowadays might be called ineluctable existential situations: facts of existence from which you cannot escape. You don't want to grow old but you can't help it. You don't want to fall sick, but it happens. You don't want to die, but die you will, like it or not. So you start asking yourself questions: 'How do I come to be in this condition? I want to go on living for ever, young and strong and healthy, but it isn't going to be that way. How is it that I have been given this urge to live when I am given not the remotest chance of escaping death? It's a riddle. But why am I presented with this riddle at all? Why this mystery? Is it God who is responsible? Is it fate? Or is this just the way it is? Is there an explanation? Or is there no explanation?'

Siddhārtha was wrestling with the fundamental questions of life and death in this way when he took in the last of the Four Sights. Riding out again in his chariot he saw a man dressed not in the usual white garb, but in a yellow robe, and shaven-headed. This man was walking calmly along the village street with a begging-bowl, going from door to door. There was something in his mindful gait that Siddhārtha found quietly compelling, and he asked the charioteer, 'What manner of man is this that looks so at peace with himself and the world?' The charioteer replied, 'This is one who has gone forth.' 'Gone forth?' said Siddhārtha. 'Gone forth from what?' 'From the world,' the charioteer explained. 'Gone forth from his home, gone forth from family. He has simply left it all behind to devote himself to the search for Truth. He's trying to find an answer to the riddle of existence. To do this he has given up all worldly ties, all domestic responsibilities, all social and political obligations. In this way he has gone forth.'[7]

You may find such people in India even today, still wearing the saffron robe. They are called sadhus, which simply means 'good people', and supporting them with alms is considered very meritorious. People give them food, invite them into their homes, and look after them. Very much the same system is still in operation after 2,500 years. And it was the sight of just such a figure that awoke in the young Siddhārtha the inspiration to go forth himself. The ultimately unacceptable limitations of human life had impressed themselves upon his consciousness too forcibly for him to be able to ignore them, to put them aside and just 'get on with his life'. You can choose not to see them, but they are there all the time, and he knew this. But now he knew also that there was a way of penetrating through to the meaning of it all. After spending a long time thinking things over, he decided that there was nothing for it but to become a sadhu himself. He felt that these questions had to be answered and that he could not rest until an answer was found.

So one full-moon night when everything was quiet, Siddhārtha bade a last farewell to his sleeping wife and child. He was not happy to leave them, but there could be no alternative. He had told no one about his decision except his faithful charioteer, who saddled the horse for him to ride out of the palace as a prince for the last time. We are told that the charioteer seized hold of the horse's tail and trotted behind, and that they travelled as far as a river marking the border of the Śākyan territory. There, Siddhārtha cut off his beard and his long, flowing black hair. Just then – it was the crack of dawn – a beggar came along, and Siddhārtha offered to swap clothes with him. It did not take the beggar long to agree to this proposal, eccentric as it seemed, and he went on his way blinking with delight at the richly embroidered robes he now wore, the gold and silver buttons and buckles on them gleaming in the first rays of the sun. Siddhārtha made his farewells to his faithful charioteer and his faithful horse, and watched them go. Then he plunged on into the jungle, alone.

He went in search of teachers who he hoped might have penetrated to the ultimate mystery of existence. In those days in India, as much as in India today, there were many who illumined the ways to the attainment of Truth. He went from one teacher to another; he practised according to their instructions and mastered what they had to teach. But he was not satisfied. Good and profound as their teachings were, he knew that there was something beyond all they knew, something beyond all they had realized. He had no name for it. He did not know what it was. But he had to find it – he had to know it. He had to carry on his search.

He was grateful for all that he had learned, but he moved on. He began a programme of terrible austerities. This was a common practice in India, as it is still today, for it was thought that the thinner the veil of the flesh, as it were, the more transparent it was to the light of the spirit. For years Siddhārtha mortified the flesh, and no one in India exceeded him in self-torture. The fame of his austerities was noised abroad, so it is said, like the sound of a great bell hung in the canopy of the sky, and he began to gather followers of his own. Eventually, however, something happened to make him wonder if he wasn't making a great deal of progress in the wrong direction. He fainted and collapsed into a river, from which, not having the strength to save himself, he was fortunate to be rescued. When he recovered he said to himself, 'This is ridiculous. I'm getting no nearer to the Truth, for all this asceticism. I've been wasting my time. It's all been a big mistake.'

So Siddhārtha Gautama the great ascetic started taking regular meals again. His five disciples were not at all impressed. The fact was that they were not so much disciples as admirers, hangers-on. They relied on him to make the effort, and just hung on to his coat-tails in the hope that his achievements would somehow rub off on them. They thought that when he achieved his goal by virtue of his austerities they would be the first to benefit. So it was obviously a great disappointment to them when he made the decision to give his body the nourishment it needed. 'He's backsliding,' they said to one another, 'He's gone back to the luxurious ways of the world. Clearly he's not the man we thought he was.' And they trooped off in disgust. Once again, Siddhārtha was on his own.

It was six years after he had left the palace when he came to the place that would mark the end of his quest. At a spot in the present-day state of Bihar called Uruvelā, now known as Buddha Gaya, he found a copse of beautiful trees beside a river. It seemed an ideal location in which to sit and meditate. Then as he sat there in the shade, with a cool breeze blowing, he remembered something that suddenly seemed to show the way forward. He recollected his experience of thirty years before, sitting beneath another tree, while his father initiated the season's ploughing. He gently felt his way back to that integrated state of concentration – not trying to force it, but just letting it come, and letting go of whatever hindered its arising. As he did so a cowherd's wife from a neighbouring village brought him some milk-rice, which he took, and he was nourished and strengthened by it. A grass-cutter also came up to provide him with a heap of kuśa grass to sit upon, and he made himself comfortable on it. Then he settled down and gave himself to his meditative experience. He plunged deeper and deeper into it, through level after level of superconscious states.

How long he sat there we do not know. It may have been days; it may have been weeks; it may even have been months. All we do know is that on the night of Vaiśākha Purnima he saw the solution to the problem upon which his mind had been bent ever since the Four Sights had awakened him to it. He not only saw this solution, but understood it, plunged into it, became one with it, and realized it. Full illumination arose within him and he became Enlightened.

Some of the early texts try to give us some idea of the content of that experience, but this is by no means an easy thing to attempt. Enlightenment is inherently ineffable. It is not to be circumscribed by the rational mind. However, to begin with, we can say that it is a state of pure, clear, radiant awareness. And it is sometimes specified that in this state of awareness one no longer makes any emotional distinction between oneself and others. That sense we have of an inner world set against the world outside ourselves is entirely transcended. There is just one continuous, pure, and homogeneous awareness extending freely in all directions. It is, moreover, an awareness of things *as they really are.* This means an awareness of things not as objects, but as transcending the duality of subject and object. Hence this pure, clear awareness is also spoken of as an awareness of Reality. It is a state of knowledge – knowledge not in the ordinary sense of someone accumulating notions of things, but rather a seeing of 'things' directly and truly, unmediated by any separate subject doing the seeing. It is a spiritual vision – even a transcendental vision – which is free from all delusion, all misconception, all wrong, crooked thinking, all vagueness, all obscurity, all mental conditioning, and all prejudice.

However, this is not the end of it. Enlightenment can be described as full illumination, as transcendental awareness, as Wisdom. But it is also an overflowing of profound love and compassion for all that lives. It is described, too, as supreme bliss, or complete emancipation – the bliss of release from the subjective ills and limitations of conditioned existence. It is thus also characterized by inexhaustible energy continually bubbling forth, total spontaneity, uninterrupted creativity. At the same time none of these aspects of Enlightenment function separately from one another. Therefore the actual experience cannot be described at all. Only by reflection on the Dharma – reflecting on the Buddha's teaching as well as on his example – by deep communication with friends, and above all by meditation, can we get some real intimation of what the Enlightenment of a Buddha consists in.

The traditional accounts say that the Buddha's Enlightenment arose or blossomed gradually as the full-moon night of Wesak wore on. According to one account, in the first watch of the night the Buddha looked back into the past, into 'the dark backward and abysm of time'.[8] He looked back over the whole course of human history, over millions of years of evolution. We are told that he was able to survey all his previous lives and see what he had done and what had arisen in consequence of his actions. He saw the conditions he had laid down and the results that had followed from them. And he saw that it was all done with, all ended. He had transcended the whole process of conditioned existence.

Then in the second watch of the night he looked, as it were, all around him, all around the universe, and he saw beings of every kind – human beings, animals, even beings in higher worlds. He saw how each one came into being, became what it was, in accordance with what it had done – in other words, how beings were reborn according to their karma. He saw this happening at every level of mundane existence, from the deepest abyss of the hell realms to the highest sphere of the gods.

Finally, in the third watch of the night, he directed his mind to the destruction of the *āsravas* – literally 'biases'. The *āsravas* are the natural biases of the mind, the deep-rooted tendency of the mind towards conditioned existence rather than towards that which is Unconditioned, towards unreality rather than towards Reality. There are three *āsravas*: the bias or inclination of the mind towards sensuous experience; the bias towards existence as a separate, ego-centred personality; and the bias towards spiritual ignorance, that is, ignorance of Reality. So he turned his mind in the purity of its concentration to the elimination of the *āsravas*, and in the morning, when the sun rose, he knew that for him the *āsravas* had been destroyed completely. Enlightenment had been attained. Siddhārtha Gautama had become the Buddha.

3

THE HIDDEN TEACHINGS OF THE BUDDHA'S EARLY LIFE

WHEN SIDDHĀRTHA GAUTAMA BECAME THE BUDDHA at the age of thirty-five, a great many things had taken place in his life, and each and every incident recorded in the early accounts of it is in some way deeply significant for us. It is not easy to select from the riches of such a unique and momentous biography; the previous chapter is no more than a summary of his progress to Enlightenment. Even from this bare outline, however, we can draw some specific principles of the Buddhist path through focusing on a few incidents. Here we will concentrate on just six: the Four Sights, the going forth from home into homelessness, the exchange of princely robes for a beggar's rags, the performance of austerities, being abandoned by companions, and the acceptance of help. Each one of these events is in substance historical, but at the same time has become the nucleus of a whole rich complex of myth and legend. Each one therefore assumes a universal significance; each one, that is to say, has a direct bearing on the condition of every evolving, or potentially evolving, human being.

First, then, let us consider the Four Sights: Siddhārtha's seeing for the first time – or as if for the first time – an old man, a sick man, a corpse, and a holy wanderer. Up to this point his father had apparently managed to seclude him from the world by occupying him with his martial exercises by day and entertaining him with singing girls and dancing girls in one of his three mansions by night. In a sense Siddhārtha had been secluded from real life, secluded even, you might say, from reality. For in Buddhist mythical literature the father sometimes represents ignorance – while the mother may represent craving (one being the more intellectual poison, and the other the more emotional source of suffering). So Siddhārtha had been hemmed in, confined, by ignorance, the universal father of those beings who live without awareness. Lacking the wider perspective, he had lived in a little world of his own. He had not known what was going on outside. He had been hardly aware that there was a world outside at all – not so as to make any difference to the way he had occupied himself, anyway. The existential reality of his situation had not yet broken in upon his little world.

You can find a different treatment of the same theme in the 'parable of the burning house' from the *Saddharma Puṇḍarīka*, or *White Lotus Sūtra*. In a huge crumbling mansion – so the parable opens – a lot of children are engrossed in their various childish games when a fire breaks out. But while the fire blazes merrily and gradually takes hold of the ancient fabric of the building, the children pay no heed to the acrid smell in the air, or the smoke curling up from under the door, or the crackle and roar of the flames and the creak and crash of falling timbers at the heart of the conflagration. They are simply not aware of the danger. They just go on amusing themselves with their toys. We are not concerned with the rest of the story here – suffice to say that the children are eventually saved.

The point of the opening of this parable hardly needs labouring. The burning house is this world, blazing with old age, disease, and death, while the children, of course, represent ourselves. The cosmos, conditioned existence itself, is on fire with existential suffering, yet we remain immersed in our trivial pursuits, our distractions and amusements. Most of us are occupied, much of the time, with matters that are simply unworthy of the attention of a moderately aware human being. Though we may catch glimpses of our real situation, of a real purpose to our existence, it is only too easy to slip back into the old ruts carved by social pressures and long habit.

Even when we are passionately absorbed in trifles, however, even as we waste our time over baubles and diversions, sooner or later something happens. One day, occupied though we may be with inconsequential personal things, something happens, something catastrophic, and our little world is shattered or so badly cracked, so badly dented, that we can never again be really comfortable living in it. It's as though we had, until then, never been born, like a chick in its egg; but suddenly our little world is broken open, and we find ourselves looking out through a crack into another, wider world. Reality has finally started to break in. We begin to see things as they really are. We feel as though we have grown up, and are no longer entranced by the toys and tales of childhood. Or it is as though we have woken from a dream. When we are immersed in our dreams, whatever happens seems as real, as vivid, as our waking experience. But when we wake up, the dream world rapidly fades. After a few minutes, or perhaps after a few hours, it is nothing, usually not even a memory. In the same way, when reality irrupts into our sleepy, cosy existence, we look back at our old life, all the old pursuits for which we have lost the appetite we once had, and we think, 'How could I have lived in that way? Was that really me? Was I really so foolish, so deluded?'

As a result of this sort of experience our behaviour changes, just as an adult behaves differently from a child. And people may notice that we're not the same as we used to be, that we've changed. They may wonder if there's not something wrong with us. 'Is anything the matter?' they will ask, not unkindly – though privately they may think we're not quite in our right mind, because we're no longer taking interest in the sort of things that we used to, no longer doing the things that other people like to do.

The event which shatters one's private world is very often unpleasant – it may be a bereavement, or the loss of a job, or being dropped by a lover, or discovering the infidelity of a spouse. On the other hand the breakthrough can come about in a more agreeable fashion – you get a sudden insight through art, perhaps, or music or poetry. Then again, it can occur through an experience that is neither pleasant nor unpleasant, nor even sudden: you just get discontented and dissatisfied. But whatever serves as the trip-wire, the experience which follows tends to be painful, disturbing, and consuming, because the old patterns are disrupted, the old moulds are broken. This is the sort of experience that Siddhārtha had, as illustrated by the Four Sights.

The second of our six incidents is the 'going forth from the home life into homelessness'. What this means in essence is that you separate yourself from what we may call 'the group'. It is not easily done, because the group, the collectivity, is the world most people inhabit most of the time. It is the world in which relationships are based on misunderstanding, on mutual exploitation and projection, in which people do not see each other as they really are, in which there is no genuine communication. But when the shell of your conditioning is broken and you catch a glimpse of a richer world beyond this narrow one, you can no longer function as a member of the group that defines who you are. You have to separate yourself from it. In the case of the Buddha he literally leaves home. He leaves parents, wife, and child, he leaves the tribe, he leaves the tribal territory, even – and he goes at night. No one can see him going. When you forsake the group, you are, metaphorically speaking, stealing away in the night, because the people in the group do not really see the person who is leaving it. They do not really know what you are doing. You are incomprehensible to them.

So how does this translate into the Buddhist path? What does it signify for those who follow in the Buddha's footsteps, for those who call themselves Buddhists? The significance of going forth is probably fairly obvious. It means that you start to dissociate yourself from the group, to resolve – to unravel – your identification with humanity as a mere collectivity. How you go about doing this depends, of course, on the nature of the group or groups to which you belong.

The group that springs to mind at once is the family – the blood group – and you leave the family when you leave home. At least, you begin to leave it when you leave home, and maybe everybody should literally leave home as soon as they are able to do so. Once you've left home in the straightforward sense of moving away, you start to get your family into perspective because you are no longer immersed in it. You begin to get a better view of your parents – just as, conversely, they get a better view of you. When you are at home with your parents you tend to think of them just as your parents, but of course they are much more than that – just as you are much more than someone's child. Seeing them simply as your mother and father you don't really see them, you don't really know them at all. But after you've moved away and stood on your own two feet for a time you are more likely to be able to see your various relations for what they are, for whatever individuality they may possess. Not only that, you can then also insist on being treated as an individual yourself, and not just as a daughter or son (or sister or nephew or whatever). It's a curious phenomenon, but when people visit their parents they very often, without being able to help it, slip back into relatively infantile attitudes – as a reaction, perhaps, to their parents slipping into corresponding parental attitudes. They accept the role of son or daughter again, they identify with that role, and thus cease to be themselves. So going forth from the family means being watchful for our own tendencies – and those of our relations – to slip into well-worn grooves whenever we come into the purlieus of family life.

The family is by no means the only group you take leave of when you go forth, however. There is also the social group. Going forth, you drop all the conventional, run-of-the-mill social activities. You are forced to recognize that parties, clubbing, and other social functions are generally quite worthless, trivial, and dull. This perception of social activities should not be confused with the antisocial pose adopted by people who are simply socially inept. The question is whether you hanker after the merry social whirl at all. If you do, it means that your individuality is not yet well enough defined to enable you to step away from the social group. However, even if you do give the more institutionalized forms of the social group a wide berth, you still find a chronic level of merely social chit-chat and gossip in most ordinary social circles. So when Siddhārtha went forth into the homeless life he was also going forth from this sort of thing – although when he became the Buddha, he found that his own Sangha was not entirely free of unmindful nattering. He even went so far as to say to his disciples on one occasion, 'When you meet together, either keep quiet altogether, or talk to some spiritual purpose, about the Dharma, about things that are helpful to your individual development.'

Then there is the economic group. You're connected with the economic group mainly through your job – if you have one. To develop as an individual, therefore, you have to avoid identifying yourself with the work you do. Unfortunately, this identification is established in common parlance: instead of saying one does this or that kind of work, one says 'I am a bricklayer,' or 'I am a stockbroker.' Not only this, but people sometimes identify very strongly with the firm they work for – and this is widely encouraged, particularly by Japanese employers – or else with a trade union. There are, of course, some jobs which are vocational, and which it may be entirely appropriate to regard as a genuine expression of creativity or compassion. That's a different matter. You may also be able to work with other Buddhists on a project or within a business which has some kind of altruistic dimension to it. In this case, too, a full personal commitment to one's work will form part of one's spiritual practice. But if one does a straightforward job as a money-generating enterprise, that is not something with which to identify oneself.

Going forth from the economic group involves, in fact – and this is an idea that goes against the flow of a major current in our conditioning –

doing as little work as possible. When you are really serious about being a Buddhist you have to make time for spiritual practice. This means, if possible, getting a part-time job. Then – and this is the difficult part – one has to resist the temptation to spend all one's spare time reading the newspaper, watching television, chatting idly, window-shopping, etc. Going forth from the economic group is all about making proper and creative use of whatever spare time you can make for yourself and dissociating yourself from whatever you do for a salary.

What we mean by 'the group' should be coming clear by now. Another quite fundamental one is the cultural group. You emancipate yourself from the cultural group into which you have been born in two different ways: by study and by travel. By studying the products of other cultures, familiarizing yourself with the literature, the music, or even the social customs of another culture, you have broadened your outlook, your sympathies. You have ceased to identify with a particular culture. Travelling on your own, or simply observing the different mores of ethnic groups within your own society, also naturally tends to loosen up your attitudes. Particularly if you can go and actually live in a completely different society, you soon realize how many of your own habits, your ways of thought, are just a product of your environment. There is no inherent validity in them at all. It is no more a basic law of the universe to eat, say, with a knife and fork than it is to eat with one's fingers.

The group is not of course necessarily a big group. What is often nowadays the most insidious type of group is the group of two – what the French call *égoïsme à deux*. The basis for what is apparently seen to be the ideal form of sexual relationship nowadays is mutual emotional dependence, mutual exploitation. And unless the sexual relationship is put in its proper place in one's scheme of things, unless it is seen as a not immensely important relationship, it cannot but hinder one's development as an individual. Unfortunately, as sexual relationships tend to be by their very nature volatile, this condition is seldom fulfilled. So this is yet another implication of going forth – leaving the group of two.

The group operates in many different ways, but these examples should suffice to give a rough idea of how we as individuals can move away from it, and an idea, therefore, of what Siddhārtha's going forth means to us in practice.

Following on from the going forth, we come to the third of our six incidents: the exchange of clothes with the beggar. Leaving home for Siddhārtha meant leaving his position in society. In those days one's position in society was signalled, to a far greater extent than it is today, by one's dress. In giving up his princely robes, Siddhārtha gave up his social identity, his identity as a Kṣatriya, as a member of the Śākya tribe. He gave it up because it was not his real identity, and he knew it, though what his real identity was he did not yet know. Ideally, perhaps, he should have gone without clothes at all, but it was later on, in his ascetic period, that he went naked. For now, he wore the clothes of a beggar, because on the social scale a beggar is nobody – he doesn't count, he doesn't exist. If you haven't got anything – no property, no money, no influence – you're nothing, nobody. Siddhārtha gave up his social identity by changing clothes with someone who had no social identity.

To use a term from Jungian psychology, Siddhārtha surrendered his persona. Persona literally means 'mask', and the term is used to refer to the psychological mask one wears when dealing with other people. Some people have many masks which they use on different occasions – and putting them on becomes an instinctive, barely conscious way of guarding themselves in any interaction they may have with another person. They wear masks because they are afraid – afraid of being seen as they are. They think people will disapprove of them if they drop the mask, that they will be rejected. Ideally, you should be able to fling aside your persona, at least with your friends, but in any case you have at least to try to be aware of your mask and thus be aware also that you are not your mask. The chief way in which people reinforce their masks is, of course, by wearing a particular style of dress or uniform. Useful as a uniform may be in assuming a necessary social role, one cannot identify oneself with that role without damaging oneself as an individual. So when Siddhārtha cast off his princely clothes he was casting off his persona, his mask.

As for his performance of austerities, the fourth event we have isolated from the Buddha's early biography, it may be difficult to imagine what possible significance this spiritual cul-de-sac – which he explored so exhaustively – might have for us. The closest most people in the West come to practising austerities is probably trying to give up smoking. Self-torture is not a spiritual error we are in any danger of falling into. However, we need to look at what was underlying Siddhārtha's practice of austerities. What was he really trying to do in pushing himself to the very limits of his endurance? In a way it's obvious. He was trying to gain Enlightenment by force of will, by sheer force of ego-directed effort. His conscious mind took the decision to realize Enlightenment, and then tried to force this decision on to the rest of his psyche. Of course, the rest of his psyche refused to co-operate in this enterprise, noble as it was, so all that effort turned out to be useless.

The point of this is not that we should stop making so much effort. That isn't it at all. The key to what he was doing when he was practising austerities lies in what happened when Siddhārtha sat down under the bodhi tree and started to meditate. What happened then was that he recollected his early mystical experience – and the significance of this experience was that it was spontaneous. It was a product of his psyche as a whole. The effort we put into our development needs to be directed towards the growth of the whole psyche, not just a part of it. We need to unify our energies, and this means enlisting the co-operation of our unconscious energies – by means of myth and symbol, and by the exercise of imagination and devotion. The rational approach will not do on its own. This is what Siddhārtha discovered when his ascetic enterprise fell through.

The fifth incident is the abandonment of Siddhārtha by his companions. They were also looking for the way to Enlightenment, but they depended on Siddhārtha to do their work for them. They wanted an easy ride in his slipstream, as it were. At the same time they had fixed ideas of how he ought to go about leading them forward; therefore their notion of how to make the best use of their association with him was quite topsy-turvy. Instead of accepting his guidance and following his example as best they could, they waited to be spoon-fed while clinging to their own views. And it has to be said that Siddhārtha's experience has a bearing on our own situation as Buddhists that we need to take into account.

Sometimes you find yourself following the same path as other people so you naturally go along together for a while. But then what if you begin to have doubts about the path you are all following? What if you want to change direction, or retrace your steps? And what if your companions disagree with your perception and think you are copping out? The hard fact is that if others are not willing to go with you, then you have to go on alone. The position may even be that you are agreed on the path but your companions are simply not willing to follow it very far, even very seriously. Then, too, you have to go on alone. This is often the position when a spiritual tradition becomes fossilized and the majority of the 'followers' of that tradition are satisfied with a more or less nominal observance of its principles and practices. If you decide to take those principles and practices rather more seriously, you are going to find yourself in a minority – perhaps in a minority of one.

The fact of the matter is that anyone who decides to become a Buddhist, to commit themselves to the principles of Buddhism – or, in the traditional idiom, to go for Refuge to the Three Jewels, to the Buddha, the Dharma, and the Sangha – is not joining a group. The Sangha, the Buddhist community, is not there to make decisions or do your thinking for you. It is a community of individuals who take full responsibility for their own actions. Only if one is ready to be on one's own is one going to be fit to be a member of the Sangha.

Our final incident, Siddhārtha's acceptance of help – milk-rice from the cowherd's wife and kuśa grass from the grass-cutter – might again seem a rather minor detail in the build-up towards his Enlightenment. However, it reflects an attitude – even a change of attitude – on the part of Siddhārtha that is actually crucial. We cannot afford to think lightly of any help we receive, however minor. Some people speak very slightingly of whatever is provided to aid spiritual practice. They say, perhaps, that shrines are not necessary, that you should be able to meditate anywhere; or they say that Buddhist scriptures are not necessary, that you should be able to discover the Truth for yourself. Well, maybe we should – but the fact is that in practice we can't. In any case, the way to Enlightenment is difficult enough already. There is no need to make it more difficult still. If Siddhārtha could accept help, we might as well do the same if we truly want to reach our goal as he did.

These, then, are the six incidents in the Buddha's progress that have a particular relevance to our own development. They are, so to speak, the hidden teachings of the Buddha's early life. Beginning with the Four Sights, we have to get a glimpse, at least, of our existential predicament, of things as they really are, of the world outside our daily concerns. In going forth from home into the homeless life, we cease to identify with the group in any of its various forms. Siddhārtha's surrender of his princely clothes represents the surrender of his persona, and we too need to look for the reality behind our masks, to disclose not just our psychological identity but our spiritual individuality. Then we have to realize, as Siddhārtha did when he renounced the way of austerity, that the conscious mind cannot impose itself on the rest of the psyche by sheer effort of will, that the hidden forces of the unconscious must be harnessed, not overborne. His companions deserting him illustrates the fact that you have to be prepared to go it alone if necessary. On the other hand, as Siddhārtha's acceptance of help should clearly signal to us, being self-reliant does not mean that we don't accept with gratitude every little bit of help we can get.

The image of an Indian prince from ancient times wandering off into the forest may seem remote, even alien, to us. However, beneath the exotic surface details of his early life there lie some fundamental patterns which we can identify in our own lives. Beneath the apparently prosaic and contingent circumstances of our own lives there are hidden teachings too. And this must surely give us confidence in our own spiritual potential. If we can recognize, in Siddhārtha's story, our own deepest strivings for ultimate liberation from the confines of conditioned existence, and the first steps we are already, perhaps, beginning to take in order to fulfil them, then we can also see that what Siddhārtha finally realized is what we too can realize, eventually, for ourselves.

4

The Heroic Ideal in Buddhism

ALTHOUGH VERY FEW PEOPLE IN THE WEST have so far had the opportunity to study or practise Buddhism to any great depth, most of us will have formed some sort of impression of it. We will have formed, too, some sort of impression of the Buddha. We meet people or we hear of people who have espoused Buddhism, we read articles about Buddhism in the newspapers, we hear people talking on the radio or the television about Buddhism – we may even, if we go to the cinema, see film stars impersonating the Buddha. Some of these impressions may be quite positive, even in some degree accurate, but inevitably there will be others which are very misleading and, once established, misconceptions are notoriously difficult to eradicate. The most persistent misconceptions derive, in fact, from the earliest Western interpreters of Buddhism, who naturally saw it from the standpoint of their own religious tradition, a Victorian version of Christianity. It was natural enough for this first wave of Western literature on Buddhism to explain it to largely Christian readers by making use of Christian concepts, but the misconceptions they generated have stood up remarkably robustly to the passage of time.

One of them, for example, was the idea that Buddhism was not a religion in the full sense of the word. According to this view it could be regarded as an impressive system of philosophy, like that of Plato, or Kant, or Hegel; or an admirable scheme of ethics; or even a system – a remarkable system – of mysticism; but as no more, really, than that. Roman Catholic scholars in particular (for some reason or other Roman Catholics have always tended to make a bit of a speciality of Buddhism) damned it with faint praise in this way and somehow suggested that there was a whole dimension missing in Buddhism which was supplied in full within Christianity.

Another equally tenacious misconception was that Buddhism was a specifically oriental religion, that it was inextricably tied up with various oriental cultures. This is evidently quite a difficult one to see through, because even today there does not seem to be a great deal of enthusiasm for the idea of distinguishing the essence of Buddhism from its cultural expression – exotic, colourful, and attractive as these expressions invariably are. But if the practice of the Buddhist path is really to be established in the West, we will have to find ways of integrating the Dharma with our own, more humdrum, grey, and familiar culture.

The particular misconception to which this chapter is addressed originated in the Victorian perception of the Buddha himself. They tended – again, naturally enough – to see him as a sort of oriental Jesus, and the popular Victorian conception of Jesus was a rather milk-and-water version of the real thing. It has been said that for the Victorians Christ was a ghostly figure in a white sheet gliding around Galilee and gently rebuking people for not believing in the Nicene Creed. So a Victorian Buddha was likewise installed in the popular imagination as a ghostly figure in a yellow sheet gliding around India and gently rebuking people for not being kind to animals.

In this way, Buddhism began to be perceived as a rather passive, negative, or gutless teaching and tradition. This impression, unfortunately, can only be reinforced, perhaps unconsciously, by any acquaintance one may have with later Buddhist art, in which decadent phase the Buddha is depicted as a sweet, dreamy, effeminate figure. As for the mass-produced representations of the Buddha that are turned out in India today – usually on calendars – their attempts at the smile of Enlightenment leave the Buddha with the coquettish simper of a sentimental starlet. Such images cannot but influence the way we see the Buddha in our own minds.

Another factor which we have to take into account is that Buddhism is a religion of Indian provenance. While Indian culture is respected for its 'spirituality' it is also looked upon as backward, slow, unprogressive, and unenterprising, and therefore epithets of this sort seem naturally to attach themselves to Buddhism when it is considered as an Indian religion.

We also have to recognize that a good deal of contemporary Buddhist teaching in the East, particularly from Sri Lanka, Burma, and Thailand, has tended to be rather negative. You are told not to do this and to refrain from that and abstain from the other, but you are not nearly so often told what you can do to cultivate positive qualities and develop in a positive sense. The oldest Buddhist scriptures recognize that you can't have one side of a coin without the other, and carry a forthright positive emphasis as well as an uncompromising negative one, but the teaching has been too often presented in the West in terms of avoidance rather than engagement, in terms of escape rather than commitment.

In order to redress this imbalance we have to take a fresh look at what Buddhism is about; we have to rethink, perhaps, our whole attitude to the spiritual life. The aim of Buddhist teaching is the attainment of Enlightenment, or Buddhahood, a state of moral and spiritual perfection, and this ideal calls for the exercise, on the moral and spiritual plane, of heroic qualities. When we speak of the heroic ideal in Buddhism, we are not speaking of anything distinct from – much less still opposed to – the spiritual ideal. We are speaking of the spiritual ideal itself – an ideal that requires heroism in the highest degree.

We are not out of the woods yet, however. It is all very well to suggest that the spiritual ideal is not just a Goody Two-shoes, keep-your-nose-clean ideal – that it is actually a heroic ideal. But how do we really feel about this 'heroic ideal'? Let's face it, the whole concept is unfashionable. The whole notion of having ideals suggests 'alienation' and lack of 'acceptance', to use the fashionable terminology. As for the hero or heroine, he or she is tainted by a suggestion of nobility, of a kind of real superiority in his or her make-up, that is somehow objectionable to modern taste.

A hundred years ago it was quite different. Victorians flaunted their high ideals with an assurance that seems unthinkable today, and the heroic ideal was all the rage. Such was the Victorian taste for hero-worship that almost anyone who had risen to some eminence in public life might be revered, even worshipped, as a hero. It was for this reason, perhaps, that the person representing their highest spiritual ideals, Jesus, should have been so ethereal a figure – to distinguish him from the more mundane objects of public adoration. Thomas Carlyle's lectures *Heroes and Hero-Worship*, first published in 1841, established as axiomatic the view that 'history is the biography of great men'. Thackeray was able to label his novel *Vanity Fair* as unique among the mass of fiction being run off the presses at the time (1848) by subtitling it *A Novel Without a Hero*.

On the mantelpiece in any home in the country you would find china figurines of highly esteemed public figures. Alfred Lord Tennyson, Florence Nightingale, Gordon of Khartoum, Gladstone, and Disraeli, were admired as pop stars are today. And no sooner were they dead than out came at least three, and sometimes six or seven, thick – one might say monumental – volumes of memoirs and letters. Victorian biographies were exercises in hagiography: they were intended to exhibit the great man in all his glory, striking the pose or attitude in which everybody wanted to remember him. This is why the great Victorians appear, even in retrospect, so very much larger than life.

The First World War was sold to the man in the street as an opportunity to be heroic himself, and it was probably the association of the heroic pose with incompetent generals and mass slaughter that rather did for the heroic ideal. Biographies became exercises in debunking, in showing how petty and ordinary so-called great men really were. The classic example of this new type of biography was Lytton Strachey's *Eminent Victorians* (1918), in which no fewer than four great Victorians suffered the indignity of being packed together in one slim volume. The Victorians themselves would have regarded this as shocking, almost indecent – like burying four people in one grave.

Today, heroes and heroines may still be found in the more commercial works of fiction (in a debased and perverted form), but rarely elsewhere, and certainly not in politics. When you recall that people used to write to Gladstone or Disraeli asking for a lock of their hair to wear in a locket round the neck, you have to admit that times have changed. It would be difficult to find someone involved in determining the important public issues of our day who might be regarded in quite this adulatory light. No doubt this is as it should be. Victorian hero-worship was certainly a bad case of projection, and their ideals can sometimes look like hypocrisy. 'No man is a hero to his own valet,' we observe sagely. However, if we replace ideals with cynicism, we deny the possibility of change. And if we take a valet's eye view of the hero, if the whole idea of the hero seems to us a little ridiculous and absurd, if we refuse to look up to someone of exceptional qualities, we deny reality as surely as the Victorians did. It means we cannot take seriously someone of extraordinary ability who has ideals, that is to say someone who is serious and cares deeply about something important.

I have introduced the concept of the hero at some length because although it is an unfashionable word in English, it translates – more accurately than any less challenging term does – one of the titles by which Siddhārtha Gautama was known after his Enlightenment. We know him as 'the Buddha', or sometimes 'the Compassionate One', but the Pali and Sanskrit texts also apply to the Buddha the epithets Mahāvīra, which means 'Great Hero', and Jina, which means 'Conqueror'. In fact, the title Jina is almost as common in the earliest Buddhist texts as the one we are so familiar with, 'the Buddha'. He is the Conqueror because he has conquered the whole of conditioned existence within himself. He has conquered the world by conquering himself. According to the *Dhammapada*, 'Though one may conquer in battle a thousand men a thousand times, yet he who conquers himself has the more glorious victory.'[9] Later, medieval Buddhism produced the idea of the Trailokya Vijaya, 'the conquest of the three worlds' – conquest, that is, of the world of sensuous desire, the world of archetypal form, and the world of no form. So the Jina's victory is over these three inner worlds.

By virtue of this conquest the Buddha becomes, of course, a king. Having subdued all the realms of conditioned existence within his own mind, he is called the Dharmarāja, 'King of the Law', or 'King of Truth'. It is as a king that the Buddha is often portrayed in Buddhist art; we know this because he is shown bearing the insignia of royalty. These insignia are actually quite curious, at least to Westerners. In Britain the corresponding insignia are, of course, the orb and sceptre, the symbols of the reigning monarch's authority. But in India, and wherever the Buddhist cultural tradition has penetrated, they comprise instead the parasol and fly-whisk.

In India in the Buddha's day an ordinary person never used a parasol or umbrella. You certainly didn't use one for keeping off the weather – you would probably have used a leaf. A real umbrella could only be used by the king or some other noble and eminent person. According to Lama Govinda this goes back to when the elder of the tribe or village used to sit under a tree in the evening with his back against the trunk, dispensing advice and settling disputes. The umbrella became, if we accept this interpretation, a sort of artificial tree held above you as you went about, as a symbol of your social position. Following this line of thought, we can link this symbolic umbrella ultimately with the cosmic tree which, in mystical terms, overshadows the whole world, the whole of existence.

The fly-whisk is a more straightforward symbol. It is made from the tail of the yak, a plume of very soft white hair, about two feet long, and very beautiful. The tail is mounted in a silver handle, and royal personages are gently fanned with it to keep off the flies. It is still used in Hindu ritual worship. There's a stage during the *āratī*, the evening worship, when the fly-whisk is waved in front of the image of the deity – Rama or Krishna or whoever it may be – because he is being treated, for the time being, as a king as well as a god.

Therefore, just as Jesus is often represented seated with the orb and sceptre in his hands to signify his divine kingship, so in Buddhist art the Buddha is depicted with an umbrella held over him – sometimes by divine beings – and with gods flanking him, equipped with fly-whisks. These symbols show that he is king of the Dharma – king, if you like, of the spiritual universe. The Buddha being king, his chief disciple, Śāriputra, was known as his Dharmasenāpati, which means – and this may be a bit of an eye-opener – 'commander-in-chief'. No, this is not the Salvation Army we are talking about here; it is indeed the Buddhist Sangha of docile repute.

This royal symbolism and military terminology are not unconnected, perhaps, with the Buddha's original social background. Being a Kṣatriya, he belonged, according to the Hindu reckoning, to the second of the four castes, the Brahmins or priestly caste coming first in terms of status. But the Kṣatriyas didn't see it like that. While the other castes accepted this ordering of the hierarchy, the Kṣatriyas regarded themselves as the top caste. This is also the way the castes are arranged whenever they are mentioned in the Pali canon, with the Kṣatriyas first. So in the early Buddhist texts the warrior is given pre-eminence, from a purely social point of view, over the priest.

We know that when Siddhārtha was growing up, Brahminism had not penetrated into Śākyan territory, so we can be fairly sure that he was educated purely and simply as a warrior – and a warrior, in a sense, he remained. There is a legend that when he became betrothed to Yaśodharā some of her kinsmen objected that he wasn't good enough at fighting, and of course he had to prove his worth by defeating them all in contest. Clearly, as a nobleman it was not enough to be a warrior – he was required to be an exceptional warrior, a hero.

It is quite significant that this should have been the background of the person who would become the prime exemplar of the spiritual life.

It is significant as well that the heroic qualities he had been trained to exhibit on the battlefield were drawn upon at every step of his spiritual quest. We know that he left home when he was about twenty-nine. He left everything he had been taught to believe in as the good life, everything he had been taught to believe was worth while, everything he had been taught to believe was his duty. It must have been a great wrench to leave his family and his tribe, to go out alone into the darkness, into the forest, going he knew not where, knowing only that he went in search of the Truth. But this is what he did.

Then for such a man to support himself as a mendicant called for no less a degree of fortitude. The traditional procedure of the almsround was simple enough, as it still is today. You take a big, black begging-bowl, and moving from door to door you stand for a few minutes at each house, and people come out and put a few scraps of food in your bowl. When you feel you've collected enough for your meal, you go off to a quiet spot outside the village and sit down to eat it. Not a demanding way of providing for oneself, you might think, but there is a rather poignant touch in the Buddha's own account of his first almsround which shows what it can be like when you aren't used to it. What he apparently told his disciples, according, that is, to the scriptures – but the story has the ring of truth to it anyway – is that the first time he sat down outside a village with his bowl, he took one look at the heap of disparate scraps of food in it and vomited. Having been used to the choicest quality of absolutely fresh food prepared by the best cooks, he found himself gazing down at the coarse leftovers of peasants and his stomach turned. But he did not allow his own delicacy to stand in the way of his quest. If the price of his freedom was to subsist on this sort of diet he had to overcome his disgust. And that is what he did.

His clothing was rough and ready too, of course. Going around the modern Buddhist world you can easily get the impression that the Buddha went around in brand new, beautifully laundered, clean and neat yellow robes, but this seems highly unlikely. He almost certainly wore rough yellow garments, stained and ragged. It's a sad fact nowadays that in some Buddhist countries a monk who goes around in a rather old robe is considered a bit of a disgrace. I myself remember coming down to a monastery in Calcutta from Kalimpong one time and – I have to say – I did not think to dress up for the occasion, but some of my monk friends were quite scandalized because I happened to be wearing a very old robe. To them it was terrible: 'What will people think?' they said. We have to imagine that the Buddha himself would have had a completely different sartorial attitude. For him, what he wore would have represented a complete break from his previous way of life, in which his secure social position was clearly reflected in the way he dressed.

Having gone forth, Siddhārtha quickly mastered the teachings that were made available to him; he did not rest on his laurels, but took his way alone again – and no man to guide him. In his old age he used to reminisce about this critical period in his life. He described how he would be in the depths of the jungle at night, when everything was dark and silent, with no one for miles around, and he would hear a twig break or a leaf fall, and a terrible panic fear and dread would come over him. Those who have practised meditation know that this can happen sometimes – fear just wells up. It isn't that there's anything objective to be afraid of particularly, and there seems to be very little you can do about it. But this is what Siddhārtha used to experience. He would be seized with a nameless terror. So how to subdue this fear and dread? What did he do to break its hold? What in fact he realized was that he had to do literally nothing. He said, 'If the fear came while I was walking up and down, I continued walking up and down. If it came while I was sitting, I continued sitting. If while I was standing it came, then I continued standing. And if I was lying down when it came, well, I continued lying down. The fear would pass away as it had arisen.' In other words he didn't try to escape it. He let it come, he let it stay there, and he let it go away. He did not suffer his mind – his essential mind – to be disturbed by it.

Though Siddhārtha took on every difficulty and adversity that lay in his way, these provided, so far, relatively minor hardships. It is a measure of his essentially heroic character, however, that he then chose to take upon himself the most arduous spiritual path he could find. Not only this, but having taken up the practice of austerities he followed that path more rigorously than any man alive at the time. He was experimenting, searching for the Truth by trial and error, and when he tried something he followed that method to the limits of his human capacity. So he went about naked, even in the bitter winters of the Himalayan foothills, with snow lying thick on the ground. He stopped using a bowl, and just took what little food he ate in his hands. He had heard it said that if you cut down your food to a few grains of rice or barley, and a little water, this would bring you to the brink of Enlightenment, so he did this. There is a terrible description in the scriptures of the emaciated state this regime brought him to, and it is the subject of a famous Gāndhāran stone carving which portrays Siddhārtha at this stage in his career as a seated figure consisting of no more than skin and bone and tendons.

It may be difficult for us to admire this sort of endeavour – it probably seems to us simply perverse. But you have to remember that he was doing it with a very clear purpose in mind, and that the consensus at that time favoured the practice of austerities as highly efficacious if you had the heart for it. Even today in India people are very much impressed by austerities. A friend of mine who was a monk at Sarnath told me once about a visit they had there from a celebrated ascetic. His disciples impressed upon the monks that their master only ate a certain kind of grain in the morning and that it had to be ready on the dot of seven o'clock. It seemed such an important point that my friend, who was the assistant abbot at Sarnath, took responsibility for seeing that their guest had what he needed. So in the morning he carried this grain to the great ascetic's room just a little before seven o'clock to make sure he got it in time, only to find he had already gone. There were still a couple of his disciples lingering about so my friend asked them for an explanation: 'Here it is – what he wanted, just when he wanted it – and he hasn't even waited for it.' The disciples replied 'Ah, that's his greatness!' I'm afraid my friend told them, quite politely, what their teacher could do with his greatness, and as you can imagine, this did not go down well. But this sort of eccentricity can attract a great deal of attention in India. Even in the West in some religious circles, eccentricity can earn you quite a little following.

So for Siddhārtha to give all this up, to give up other people's expectations of him, to go back once again to being a nobody, required psychological and spiritual courage of a high and heroic order. It is so much easier to do anything, however difficult in itself, when you've got other people around, idolizing and applauding you, saying, 'Look at him, how heroic he is!' But when no one likes what you are doing and your admirers flounce off in disgust, that is a very testing time, and there are very, very few people who can handle it. Jesus, you might say, had something of this experience in the garden of Gethsemane.

Finally, having realized for himself what the true path was – that it led through the stages of meditation – Siddhārtha fixed his resolve on the goal with an unshakeable resolution. At this point a beautiful and dramatic verse is put into his mouth by some early compilers of the scriptures: 'Let blood dry up, let flesh wither away, but I shall not stir from this spot till Enlightenment be attained.'[10] He did not say, 'Well,

I'll give this a go for a few days, and if it doesn't work, I'll just have to try something else, I suppose.' His commitment, once he had seen the way clear before him, was total and uncompromising. Nothing less would do for the purpose he had set himself, which was to overturn conditioned existence itself. The Buddha's Enlightenment is therefore very often described in simple heroic terms as a victory – a victory over Māra, the Buddhist embodiment of evil. The name 'Māra' literally means 'Death', and he personifies all the forces of evil existing within our own mind, our negative emotions, our psychological conditionings and so on, everything that binds us to repeated suffering – in short, our craving, our hatred, and our ignorance. And on account of his victory over Māra, another of the Buddha's titles is Mārajit, the conqueror of Māra.

Given that the Buddha's attainment of Enlightenment was so conspicuously the expression – the ultimate expression – of the heroic ideal, it is no surprise to find that his teaching puts such a stress on self-reliance, on not relying even on him. There is a famous exhortation from the Buddha that appears a number of times in the Pali scriptures: 'All that a teacher could do have I done for you. Here are the roots of trees. Sit down, meditate – the rest is up to you.'[11] He was always on at the monks, asking them what they were up to, how they were getting on, never letting them slacken off, always arousing them, inspiring them, to greater efforts. And they responded – most of them. Others got a bit tired of it all, and jibbed at the pace at which the Buddha was driving them – but they soon left to find an easier teacher.

The Buddha knew from personal experience that it was no easy matter. On more than one occasion he spoke of the spiritual life in terms of a battle and addressed the monks in martial strain: 'We are Kṣatriyas, warriors,' he told them. And he did not mean that they were of the Kṣatriya caste, because his disciples were from every caste, from Brahmins to Untouchables (caṇḍālas), and no distinction of caste was respected in the Sangha. He said, 'We are warriors because we are fighters. And what do we fight for? We fight for śīla, the ethical life; we fight for samādhi, higher consciousness; we fight for prajñā, Wisdom; and we fight for vimukti, complete spiritual emancipation.' In passages like this the Buddha comes across as the embodiment of fearlessness and self-confidence. There is no false humility or bravado about him. His utterance is spoken of as his Siṁha-nāda, his Lion's Roar. We all know people who bleat like sheep, even people who 'baa' like little woolly lambs, and we know people who bark or yap like dogs. But the

Buddha's preaching is likened to the roaring of a lion because, according to Indian mythology, when the lion roars every other beast in the jungle falls silent. When the Buddha expounds the Truth, no one can stand against it.

You don't have to cast your net very wide to find the heroic ideal being extolled or put into practice in the Buddhist scriptures. However, for a more direct and immediate impression of the fundamentally heroic nature of the Buddhist ideal, you have only to look at some of the more powerful images in Buddhist art. I am not thinking here of the Gāndhāran tradition of sculpture, which is not purely Indian and is sometimes a bit cloying, but of the Mathura tradition, named after a place not very far from where Delhi is today, and the earliest purely Indian art, in which is emphasized vigour rather than gentleness, confidence rather than tenderness, strength rather than sweetness. Characteristic of this artistic movement is a standing portrayal of the Buddha as a powerfully-built man in the prime of life, firmly erect, like a great tower or a massive tree, and making with his hands the *abhaya mudrā* – the gesture of fearlessness.

Buddhist art does not, of course, focus solely on the Buddha himself, nor is the heroic ideal embodied solely in the person of the Buddha. From the Mahāyāna development of Buddhism emerged, as its most important contribution to the Buddhist vision, the figure of the Bodhisattva. As an archetype, the Bodhisattva became a symbolic manifestation of a particular aspect of Enlightenment; and one of the most important and revered of these archetypal Bodhisattvas is Mañjuśrī, who represents Wisdom. Just as in the *Dhammapada* the Buddha describes the Dharma-farer as destroying the hosts of Māra with the sword of Wisdom, so Mañjuśrī is depicted – in the form known as Arapacana Mañjuśrī – as brandishing aloft in his right hand a flaming sword, the sword of knowledge, or Wisdom. Later still in the historical development of Buddhism, the central figure of Tantric Buddhism is the figure of the wrathful Vajrapaṇī, who represents, in his graphically fearsome aspect, the heroic, fearless energy of the Enlightened mind. In his right hand he brandishes a *vajra*, an indestructible weapon of irresistible power.

The Bodhisattva ideal, the determination to guide all sentient beings to nirvāṇa, is the epitome of the heroic ideal as exemplified in the Buddha's own life. In the Mahāyāna literature the Bodhisattva is likened to the new moon: as the new moon is to the full moon so the Bodhisattva is to the Buddha. As the new moon waxes to full moon so the Bodhisattva grows towards Buddhahood, and he or she does this by the practice of the six *pāramitās*, the six transcendental virtues of generosity, ethics, patience, energy, meditative concentration, and Wisdom. These virtues are all to be practised, according to the Mahā-yāna texts, on a truly heroic scale. It's not just a matter of an occasional burst of generosity, a momentary awareness of the ethical dimension in one's choice of action, a reasonable degree of patience, a fitful stirring of spiritual energy, a modicum of meditative absorption once or twice a week, and the odd moment of reflection and contemplation on the Dharma.

Take generosity, for instance. The Bodhisattva gives not just material things, but even life and limb if necessary. It is against this sort of background that we can understand the self-immolation of Vietnamese monks who wanted to draw attention to the terrible spiritual plight of their country. And the Bodhisattva practises all the virtues or perfec-tions, not just during one lifetime, but (according to the heroic vision of Mahāyāna Buddhism) over an enormous number of lives spanning three *kalpas*, or aeons.

The Bodhisattva as hero is delineated particularly clearly in a passage from the *Aṣṭasāhasrikā*, the 'Perfection of Wisdom in 8,000 Lines'. As usual in the *Prajñāpāramitā* sūtras, the Buddha is addressing his disciple Subhūti:

> Suppose, Subhūti, that there were a most excellent hero, very vigorous, of high social position, handsome, attractive and most fair to behold, in possession of all the finest virtues, of those virtues which spring from the very height of sovereignty, morality, learning, renunciation and so on. He is judicious, able to express himself, to formulate his views clearly, to substantiate his claims; one who always knows the suitable time, place and situation for everything. In archery he has gone as far as one can go. He is successful in warding off all manner of attack, most skilled in all arts, and foremost, through his fine achievements, in all crafts. He has a good memory, is intelligent, clever, steady and prudent, versed in all the treatises, has many friends, is wealthy, strong of body, with large limbs, with all his faculties complete, generous to all, dear and pleasant to many. Any work he might undertake he manages to complete. He speaks methodically, shares his great riches with the many, honours what should be honoured, reveres what should be revered, worships what should be worshipped.

Would such a person, Subhūti, feel ever increasing joy and zest?

Subhūti: He would, O Lord.

The Lord: Now suppose, further, that this person, so greatly accomplished, should have taken his family with him on a journey, his mother and father, his sons and daughters. By some circumstances they find themselves in a great, wild forest. The foolish ones among them would feel fright, terror and hair-raising fear. He, however, would fearlessly say to his family: 'Do not be afraid! I shall soon take you safely and securely out of this terrible and frightening forest. I shall soon set you free!' If then more and more hostile and inimical forces should rise up against him in that forest, would this heroic man decide to abandon his family, and take himself alone out of that terrible and frightening forest – he who is not one to draw back, who is endowed with all the forces of firmness and vigour, who is wise, exceedingly tender and compassionate, courageous and a master of many resources?

Subhūti: No, O Lord. For that person, who does not abandon his family, has at his disposal powerful resources, both within and without. On his side forces will arise in that wild forest which are quite a match for the hostile and inimical forces, and they will stand up for him and protect him. Those enemies and adversaries of his, who look for a weak spot, will not gain any hold over him. He is competent to deal with the situation, and is able, unhurt and uninjured, soon to take out of that forest both his family and himself. And securely and safely they will reach a village, city or market-town.

The Lord: Just so, Subhūti, is it with a Bodhisattva who is full of pity and concerned with the welfare of all beings, who dwells in friendliness, compassion, sympathetic joy and impartiality.[12]

This, then, is an account, from the *Prajñāpāramitā* tradition, of the Bodhisattva as hero, leading all sentient beings out of the deep forests of saṃsāra to the city of Enlightenment. If we turned to other traditions – Zen, or Tantric Buddhism – we could produce many other examples of the heroic ideal in Buddhism. But perhaps enough has been said to dismiss the notion of Buddhism as a disengaged, bloodless, or effete teaching and tradition. We may say, on the contrary, that it asserts the heroic ideal to a degree that ought to render it quite unfashionable. And as Buddhists we should be prepared to question fashionable ideas and attitudes. To a Buddhist it must seem a pity that the heroic ideal has been discredited or degraded in our century, because people really need something to live for, and, if necessary, to die for. So fundamental, indeed, is it to Buddhism, that we may say that the heroic ideal is conterminous with the spiritual life itself. Heroism is intrinsic to the quest for Enlightenment, and it therefore runs to the very core of the essential nature of the Buddha.

5

FROM HERO-WORSHIP TO THE WORSHIPPING BUDDHA

IF THE BUDDHA IS, by his very nature, a hero, and if the Buddhist ideal is a heroic ideal, where does this leave us? How does the heroic ideal relate to us, or how do we relate to it? What is the difference between one who is a hero and one who is not a hero? Is there an *essential* difference between them? It might help to answer this if we bring in another term here, if we say that the hero is also the genius – the cultural hero. So where does the difference between the genius and the ordinary person lie? The way we use the term 'genius' tends to suggest that the difference is one of kind, that the genius is somehow a different species, but in fact the difference is simply one of degree. It is as though what is undeveloped or hardly developed in ourselves is highly developed or fully developed in someone we call a genius.

Take music, for instance, which is a series of sounds organized in such a meaningful pattern as to be beautiful. Clearly, anyone who is not deaf has, in some degree, the capacity to appreciate it. Dr Johnson used to confess, or rather – more characteristically – used to pride himself on the fact, that he was unable to recognize the tune to *God Save the King*. It is questionable, however, whether the musical faculty can really be *totally* missing from a person's make-up. In the case of a great musician that faculty is simply – by virtue of an innate or developed predilection, sheer application, parental encouragement, natural talent, and force of character – converted into what we call genius. The same goes for literature. A great poet or novelist uses the same mode of expression as we do when we write a letter, only they take their use of language to the highest possible pitch of expressiveness. And it is said that the most wretchedly painted signboard of a village inn shows that a Rembrandt once lived in the world.

This principle may be applied to almost any subject. Some people are good philosophers and others are poor philosophers, but no one can be said to be without a philosophy at all. A great philosopher simply philosophizes with greater rigour and imagination than the rest of us. If the difference between the genius and the ordinary person were a matter not simply of degree, but, in some sense, of kind, we should be unable to appreciate the productions of genius. We can appreciate the music, or the poetry, or the philosophy, only because there is music and poetry and philosophy already in us. We have an affinity – however undeveloped – for these things. One of the medieval German mystics, in a poem, compares the affinity of the eye with the sun to the affinity of the human soul with God. Just as the eye could not behold the sun unless the eye had in it something that was like the sun, he says, so the human soul could not perceive the divinity unless in the human soul there was something of the divine. So we cannot appreciate Mozart unless there is something of Mozart in us. We cannot appreciate Shakespeare unless there is something of Shakespeare in us. And, as we shall see, we cannot appreciate the Buddha unless there is something of the Buddha in us.

Such appreciation does not come easily, of course. We may be stretched and challenged to our limits by the output of a creative artist. Indeed, it may be beyond us altogether to appreciate their work. Even in the case of Mozart, who is not commonly regarded as a revolutionary, some of his contemporaries thought they detected in his later works mistakes of harmony, whereas in fact he had simply moved beyond the conventions of the time. He had outstripped the general level of sensibility. To begin with, the creative genius is on his or her own, but then gradually more and more individuals catch up with their vision, until eventually there is a general raising of cultural sensibility. Almost anyone becomes able, with a little effort, to appreciate the work of great individuals of the past.

A corresponding process takes place in the opposite direction. The general level of cultural achievement provides the raw materials with which the exceptional individual expresses his or her genius. It is no coincidence that Mozart grew up in an intensely musical society, or that Michelangelo appeared at the height of the Italian Renaissance, or that Shakespeare honed his skills amidst a galaxy of dramatic poets, or that Plato cogitated within a city humming with philosophical inquiry. The same must go for the originators of spiritual and religious traditions. They are the product, in some degree, of favourable cultural milieux, and it is no surprise to find that the Buddha appeared at a time of intense spiritual inquiry. Cultural development, however, takes place largely through the efforts of individuals working on their own or in contact with a few friends. Groups, schools, and institutions tend to stifle creativity.

In terms of cultural evolution, then, the genius or the hero is the forerunner, a few steps ahead of the rest of humanity, but leading the way for others to follow. This brings us back to our evolutionary model of human development: on the one hand we have the Buddhist model of spiritual development, and on the other we have the scientific model of evolution. As we have seen, the two models may, from a Buddhist viewpoint at least, be put together, so that the Buddhist vision can be seen as in some sense developing on from the scientific vision to produce one continuous process of development. So we start with the 'lower evolution', governed by a 'cyclic', reactive, or unconscious conditionality, and we develop by a 'spiral' principle, constituting creative, conscious action, on to the 'higher evolution'.

If we accept this overall scheme, we can then break it up into stages. First there is the subhuman stage of biological evolution. Then the specifically 'human' stage starts with the point at which self-consciousness emerges. Following on from this, the higher evolution opens with the 'superhuman' stage, characterized by the heroic individual or the genius. Finally, there is the stage starting from the point at which Insight into the nature of Reality is sustained at a sufficiently deep level to direct the individual's consciousness irreversibly towards Enlightenment. This point is traditionally called 'Stream Entry', and it marks the beginning of what we may call the 'trans-human' stage.

We can, therefore, see what our general position is. People are at a wide range of levels of development between the human stage and the superhuman. As Buddhists our agenda is to progress from wherever we are towards and through stage three, the stage of heroism and genius. So this can be something of a surprise: that our path lies not in the direction of a slow attenuation of the self, of an abandonment of the self, but rather in the direction of a strong and heroic individuality. After all, if there is one thing that distinguishes the hero and the genius from comparatively ordinary people it is their individuality. They are not units in a mass. They stand alone.

One likes to think that one is an individual, but most of the time one is not. One may even try very hard to be different – one may try to look different, behave differently, behave outrageously, indeed – but even this will not confer individuality on one (though it may, in some cases, be a start). We have to recognize that there is very little individuality about, because there is very little real awareness about, and that to become truly individual we need to make a conscious effort to become more aware: to become more deeply aware of ourselves, more deeply aware of others, more deeply aware of the environment, of what is around us, and more deeply aware of Reality itself.

Statistically, numerically, we may be individuals, but very, very few of us are individuals in a psychological and spiritual sense. Most people are simply not sufficiently aware to be classed as real individuals. So when Buddhists talk about going beyond the 'self' and realizing the truth of 'non-self', they are talking about something that is quite out of the question for most of us. Most of us have not even developed a self yet, never mind realizing the non-self. If one has not developed a self that is distinguishable from a group mentality, if one's self is little more than an amorphous mass of conditionings, if one has not yet learned to be truly oneself, then nothing is really there to transcend. It is for this reason that the Buddhist path goes by way of the kind of ardent dedication and vision – the individuality – we find demonstrated by the great artist, the genius, and the hero.

If we know who or what we mean by a hero or genius, we can get a clearer idea of what a Stream Entrant is, and even what it means to speak of a Buddha. We may say that the genius, the cutting edge of a culture – the cultural hero – represents, to a greater or lesser degree, what the average person can become, from the point of view of cultural development. The Stream Entrant then represents what this kind of true individual can become spiritually. And the Buddha represents the goal towards which the Stream Entrant is irrevocably bound. They together constitute one continuous process of development within the higher evolution.

We can thus begin to see an analogy – and perhaps not just an analogy but a real correspondence – between the cultural hero and the Buddha. The Buddha is the first historical example of what all men, all women, potentially are. The Buddha is different from other beings not in kind, but in degree of development, in the degree to which he manifests his inner potentiality. In the scriptures this crucial point is made by way of a typically homely image: 'Suppose', the Buddha says, 'a hen has laid a number of eggs, and suppose the hen sits on these eggs patiently, until they start hatching. What happens then?' Clearly, the chicks don't all hop out simultaneously. 'What happens is that one egg hatches first. So when this first chick emerges and stands clear of the eggshell, what does it do? It starts tapping with its little beak on the other shells, helping the other chicks out into the world.'

The meaning of this simile is not difficult to fathom. The egg is the state of unawareness, the womb of spiritual darkness and ignorance within which we sleep. The Buddha is the first chick, the first to break out of his shell, and having done so he then rouses the others, tapping vigorously on their shells. Maybe he hears a muffled tapping coming back at him, and he taps more vigorously, to be answered again by a more eager tapping from within until the shell cracks and a fellow chick hops out.

Yet another of the Buddha's titles, therefore, is Lokajyeṣṭha. The common translation, 'World-honoured One', does not give the full flavour of this term, because *jyeṣṭha* really means 'first-born son', and it is still used colloquially by the Nepalese in this sense. They tend to have a great many children – ten or a dozen is quite common – and they usually address them as 'first son', 'second son', 'third son', etc., and likewise with the daughters. There is a special name for each: jettha (first son), kaila (second son), maila (third son) etc. So, *loka* meaning 'world', Lokajyeṣṭha means the first-born of the world, the elder brother of humanity, and it refers to the first human being to be spiritually reborn. This means that the only difference, spiritually speaking, between the Buddha and his Enlightened disciples (the question is explicitly raised and answered in the scriptures) is that he attained Enlightenment first, by himself, whereas they attained it subsequently with his help.

In the scale of the higher evolution, the Buddha appears at the apogee – not a finite point, but, as it were, an infinite extension – of the trans-human stage. He is neither human, strictly speaking, nor even superhuman, but simply fully Enlightened. However, the higher evolution does not exclude the lower evolution; the Buddha is still human, still a man – only, at the same time, something more than that, something more, even, than a superman.

But now what, you may ask, is this idea of the 'superman' doing, coming into a discussion of the Buddha? Are we trying to interpret Buddhism along Nietzschean lines? In fact, there is no need to bring in Nietzsche here. The 'superman' or *Mahāpuruṣa* was evidently a quite important idea in India during the Buddha's lifetime, and an entire sutta, the *Lakkhaṇa Sutta*, is devoted to a full description of this ideal figure. The characteristics – *lakkhaṇa* in Pali – of the *Mahāpuruṣa* (Pali *Mahāpurisa*) amount to thirty-two major marks or signs, and eighty-four minor ones, and they quite clearly embody the highest aesthetic, cultural, and religious ideals of the time. It would seem that the Buddha was regarded by his contemporaries as conforming to this ideal of the superman, which is really quite significant because it shows that the Buddha did not bypass human perfection, even physical perfection, but incorporated it into the higher perfection of Enlightenment.

We like to distinguish human beings from animals, but in fact humanity does not exclude the animal. Our nature incorporates the animal in subordination to the truly human in us. We develop our humanity, all our truly human characteristics and functions, qualities, and attitudes, not so much by rejecting the animal as by integrating the animal into the human. Therefore, just as human beings, even at the highest pitch of their development, include the animal in their make-up, so Buddhahood includes and integrates the human in subordination to the Enlightened personality.

The point to grasp from all this is that cultural attainment and spiritual development are strictly analogous, that they represent the lower and the higher levels of an overall spiritual process, the higher evolution. They are both the work of *individuals*, in advance of, and helping, the rest of humanity. To get anywhere ourselves, then, we really do have to acknowledge that there are men and women who are more developed than we at present are. Hero-worship, or the hero-worshipping attitude, is by no means a bad thing, provided it is directed at the right objects – provided, that is to say, it is directed towards those who are really more highly developed than the rest of us, rather than towards the media-generated icons of contemporary popular culture. The tendency to cynicism, a determination to uncover the feet of clay, must be seen for what it is – a vice. That unwillingness to believe in anything like high ideals, to respect those who devote their lives to the serious pursuit of those ideals, or to recognize greatness in an individual – this whole attitude is soul-corroding and spiritually corrupt.

By contrast, Buddhists try to cultivate a spirit of admiration, of respect, of reverence and devotion. This reverence is not only for certain individuals as they are, on account of the level of spiritual development they have already attained, but also for everybody else, on account of what they are capable of becoming. A comparison is drawn in the scriptures with the convention in a monarchical system of respecting the heir to the throne even as a baby. Though this child may be playing with his rattle now, you know that one day he is going to be king, and thus you treat him with the reverence due to a king. Buddhism encourages such an attitude, such a feeling, towards all sentient beings. They may be anything now – they may be thieves or prostitutes or financiers – they may even be politicians, but one day they are going to be Buddhas. However degraded their present condition, however limited their outlook, however enmeshed they are in their own evil deeds, you need to respect them on account of what they are in potentiality, which one day will surely be realized.

No case is so desperate that you can ever say, 'Oh well, they will never get out of the hell they have created for themselves.' The classical villain of the Buddhist scriptures, for example, is Devadatta, the Buddha's cousin. In some ways he was one of the brightest of the Buddha's disciples – he had all sorts of psychic powers – but he was ambitious and jealous. One day he went to the Buddha and said, 'Lord, you are getting old. Lord, don't exert yourself any more. Take it easy, retire. I shall look after everything for you. I shall lead the Sangha.'[13] When the Buddha made it plain what he thought of this idea, Devadatta tried to initiate a split in the Sangha, which is regarded in Buddhism as a truly heinous crime. When this failed he even made attempts upon the Buddha's life. He had a mad elephant let loose upon his teacher on one occasion, and another time he sent a boulder rolling down a hill towards him. All these attempts failed, of course, and some time later Devadatta died of disappointment – and we're told that after his death he went to an unpleasant place. But the Mahāyāna scriptures tell us what Devadatta's name will be when he becomes a Buddha, and exactly when this will be. So whether or not you accept the precision of these forecasts, the principle is clear. Even someone like him has the seed of Buddhahood in him, and when he has purified himself he too will become Enlightened and liberate other sentient beings. No one, therefore, is ever completely and hopelessly lost. If Devadatta can bounce back, anyone can.

Buddhists revere their spiritual teachers in particular, because their teachers represent what they can become, what they want to become, what indeed they will become when they have made the necessary effort. If we have no reverence for our ideals as embodied in the form of human beings, whether still alive or long dead, whether we meet them through personal contact or through the pages of a book, it will hardly be possible for us to attain that ideal for ourselves. Devotional practice, the whole question of worship in Buddhism, has to be understood as proceeding from this basis.

This means that we have to dissociate the word 'worship' from notions of churchgoing and the doxologizing of a universal creator figure. It is easy for people who associate religion exclusively with the worship of God to jump to the conclusion that if Buddhists worship they must be worshipping a god. The confusion arises out of the limited sense in which the word 'worship' is used nowadays. In India, by contrast, one word serves to denote the respect you pay to anyone, whether to the Buddha, your parents, your elder brothers and sisters, your teachers – spiritual and secular – or to any senior and honourable person.

When Buddhists bow down and make offerings of flowers, candles, and incense to the image of a Buddha or a Bodhisattva, they are honouring the Buddha as an Enlightened being, not worshipping him as a god. Nor should this fact be allowed to suggest that worship plays a minor or even dispensable role in Buddhism, as those who present Buddhism as merely a rational philosophy would like to think. The expression of gratitude, of rejoicing, of respect – in short, worship – is fundamental to Buddhism. Just how fundamental becomes startlingly apparent when we take up again the account of the Buddha's life and find out what it was that occupied the Buddha's thoughts as he sat by the River Nerañjarā after his Enlightenment.

He remained in the same area for some seven weeks after attaining Enlightenment, sitting beneath the trees – a few days beneath one tree, then a few days beneath another. In this way the weeks passed by, and during this time he hardly bothered to eat. There is just one reference to food in the scriptural account – apparently, two wandering merchants offered him some honey and rice cakes – but we can assume that he was above all bodily considerations.

It wasn't just that he had gained Enlightenment. That was a tremendous thing in itself, but it wasn't just that. He had something else to do, something which was if anything even more difficult. For seven weeks he was intent upon the task of absorbing the Enlightenment experience, allowing it to transform and transmute every atom and fibre of his being. After all, what had happened to him was literally the most tremendous thing that can possibly happen to a human being. The transformation from an unenlightened to an Enlightened being is so overwhelming that, in a sense, when one becomes Enlightened, one ceases to be, in the ordinary sense, a human being at all. An Enlightened human being, a Buddha, has entered an entirely new and different category of existence.

The Buddha was the first in the course of human history to undergo this transformation. No wonder that he was staggered by his own achievement. And it seems that he found himself faced with one or two dilemmas – or, at least, certain teachings have been presented in the form of dilemmas that exercised the newly awakened mind of the Buddha. One of them is quite well known and forms the basis for the next chapter. The other, which we are going to look at now, has been almost completely overlooked by commentators on the life of the Buddha. So far as I know, no one has remarked on the extraordinary and clear implications of the passage. Both episodes are found in the *Samyutta Nikāya*, 'The Book of the Kindred Sayings' – that is, sayings of the Buddha on the same subject – but the first is found elsewhere in the Pali canon as well. The more obscure – though as we shall see, quite surprising – dilemma comes straight after the more famous one in the text, but it actually happened before it, having apparently occurred five weeks after the Enlightenment.

The Buddha's reflections at this point – the quandary he was pondering – went as follows: 'It is ill to live paying no one the honour and obedience due to a superior. What recluse or Brahmin is there under whom I could live, paying him honour and respect?'[14] Now this is surely remarkable. The Buddha has just attained supreme Enlightenment – and here we find him wondering to whom he can pay honour and respect. These days, of course, no one generally wants to pay honour and respect to anyone. We *demand* respect; we demand equality; we want to make sure that no one is regarded as superior to anyone else. Some of us may try to be polite and courteous, but the idea that respect benefits the person who offers it rather than the person to whom it is offered runs right against the grain of current social values. Not only that, the Buddha's attitude also seems to upset traditional Buddhist ideas about the Buddha, and even about Enlightenment itself.

But let us continue with the episode. Perhaps things will become a little clearer. The Buddha continues to reflect, and his reflections are concerned with four things: the training in ethics, the training in meditation, the training in insight or wisdom, and the training in contemplation of knowledge of emancipation. What he sees is that there is no one in the universe – no one among the gods, even Brahmā Sahampati, lord of a thousand worlds, and no human being, no holy or wise man anywhere – who is more accomplished in these things than he is himself. He sees that in terms of spiritual insight and under-standing he himself is the highest living being in the universe. This is how the Buddha sees himself, and if we don't see the Buddha in this way, then we don't really see the Buddha at all.

Having realized for the first time who he really is, the Buddha sees that there is no one 'under whom he can live, paying him honour and respect'. That, surely, is clear enough. One lives 'under' someone in order to learn from them. As the Buddha is more highly developed than any other living being, he has nothing to learn, spiritually speaking, from anyone. But the crucial point here is that he doesn't give up. He still requires a focus for his devotion. So he reflects further: 'This Dharma, then, wherein I am supremely Enlightened – what if I were to live under it, paying it honour and respect?' And at this very moment, Brahmā Sahampati appears before him and approves of the Buddha's decision, telling him that all the Buddhas of the past lived under the Dharma, honouring and respecting it, and that all the Buddhas of the future will do likewise.

This is really an astonishing episode. It shows that even a Buddha 'needs' (not that the Enlightened mind can be literally in need of anything) to honour and respect something. Even a Buddha needs to offer worship. So worship is not just a spiritual practice to be taken up as a means to an end, and then discarded once Enlightenment is attained. Worship is an integral part of the Enlightenment experience itself. The Enlightened mind is a worshipping mind no less than it is a realized mind or a compassionate mind. We are all familiar with the image of the meditating Buddha; we have probably seen images of the teaching Buddha, and even the standing or the walking Buddha. But we must add to these the much less familiar image of the worshipping Buddha.

The text tells us that the object of the Buddha's devotion is the Dharma – only it is not, in this case, the Dharma as we usually think of it. It is not the Dharma in the sense of the Buddha's teaching which the

Buddha worships. For one thing, by the time of this particular episode the Buddha had not, as yet, taught anybody anything. The Dharma referred to here is the Dharma as *principle*, the Dharma as the Law, the Truth, or Reality. The Dharma we know about is the Dharma as just a conceptual formulation – expressed in accordance with people's needs – of the Dharma as Reality itself. What the Buddha worships is the object or content of his own experience of Enlightenment.

When we think about it, however, a further difficulty confronts us here. If you worship something, what you worship is necessarily higher than you are. If the Buddha worships the Dharma, then the Dharma is higher than the Buddha. But in what sense can this be the case? Has not the Buddha penetrated the Dharma, mastered it, so to speak? What is left for him to worship in the Dharma? To solve this puzzle we shall have to take another, closer look at the most fundamental formulation of the Dharma, *pratītya-samutpāda*: 'conditioned co-production' or 'dependent origination'. As we saw in the first chapter, this principle consists in the fact that one thing is conditioned by something else, that whatever happens takes place by way of a cause. And conditioned co-production is of two kinds, one being a circular process symbolized by the Wheel of Life, and the other generating a spiral of spiritual development. The first of these the Buddha has clearly left behind him: he is free of the Wheel of Life. What we are concerned with at this point is *pratītya-samutpāda* in its spiral form, the form of the successive stages of the spiritual path.

The best-known formulation of this sequence of positive mental states or experiences, known as the chain of positive *nidānas*, runs as follows:

In dependence on suffering arises faith. In dependence on faith arises joy. In dependence on joy arises rapture. In dependence on rapture arises calm. In dependence on calm arises bliss. In dependence on bliss arises concentration. In dependence on concentration arises knowledge and vision of things as they really are. In dependence on knowledge and vision of things as they really are arises dispassion. In dependence on dispassion arises withdrawal, or disentanglement. In dependence on withdrawal, or disentanglement, arises freedom. In dependence on freedom arises knowledge of the destruction of the *āsravas*, or all unskilful, negative states.

So this sequence is the second of the two processes by which the principle of *pratītya-samutpāda* works out, and it represents the rationale of the spiritual life. In turn, it also divides into two sections: one mundane, the other transcendental. The first section consists of the first seven nidānas, or links, up to 'the arising of knowledge and vision of things as they really are'. All these nidānas except the seventh are – though positive, though skilful – still mundane. They are mundane because after having attained them you can still fall back to the Wheel. From 'the arising of knowledge and vision of things as they really are' onwards, however, through the five links that comprise the second section of the 'spiral', you cannot fall back – you can only go forward. And you cannot fall back from them because they are transcendental attainments.

This makes the seventh nidāna the crucial one. The arising of 'knowledge and vision of things as they really are' marks the transition from the mundane to the transcendental. It constitutes the arising of transcendental Insight, or Stream Entry – that is, it is the point at which you enter the stream that leads unerringly to the ocean of nirvāṇa. It is also, for obvious reasons, known as 'the point of no return'.

So much for the twelve positive nidānas. The reason the whole matter of the nidāna chain has been brought up is to clear up the mystery of how it is the Buddha worships the Dharma as higher than himself. The culmination of the nidāna chain is the arising of knowledge of the destruction of the *āsravas*. This is what happens when one attains Enlightenment. At this point one becomes a Buddha. But is it literally the culmination? Is the twelfth nidāna literally the last one? To answer this question we have only to turn to the scriptural account of the occasion when this nidāna chain was originally delineated. We will find that it was put forward by the brilliantly gifted nun, Dhammadinnā, whose exposition, we should add, the Buddha assented to in full.[15] From what she said it is clear that the formulation of the twelve positive nidānas stops at this point simply because it has to stop somewhere. So the implication is that there is no reason why the spiral process should not continue indefinitely. In other words, attaining Enlightenment does not mean achieving a fixed, determinate state, however high. It means becoming involved in an irreversible and unmeasured transcendental process.

Therefore, even though the Buddha was the highest living being in the universe, even though he had progressed further along the spiral path than anyone else, there were still reaches of that path, there were still developments of that progression, which he had yet to explore. This is why it was possible for the Buddha 'to live under the Dharma, paying it honour and respect'. The Dharma here is the law, or reality, of *pratītya-samutpāda*. And for the worshipping Buddha, the Dharma is especially this law or reality as represented in unnamed and as yet unrealized nidānas – nidānas which from our point of view are literally inconceivable. So this fact, that one of the first things the Buddha thinks of when he has gained Enlightenment is to look for something to worship, and that even he is able to find something to worship, should be enough in itself to convince us of the central importance of worship within Buddhism.

In this episode from the *Saṁyutta Nikāya*, the word for 'honour and respect' is *gārava*, which means, according to the dictionary, 'reverence, respect, honour, esteem, veneration, worship'. So the term clearly suggests the kind of positive attitude which we naturally adopt towards something or someone we see or experience as being higher than ourselves. Obviously there are the Buddhas and Bodhisattvas – but is there anything else that can be an object of honour and respect?

As it happens, the Buddhist tradition provides a list of six gāravas, six objects that are worthy of reverence, respect, and worship. They are: Satthā, Dharma, Sangha, *sikkhā, appamāda*, and *paṭisanthāra*. The first three of these can be more or less taken as read: they are known collectively as the Three Jewels. The central act of becoming a Buddhist, and of affirming one's commitment to Buddhism, is traditionally termed 'Going for Refuge to the Three Jewels', usually abbreviated to just 'Going for Refuge'. So you go for Refuge to the Buddha as the ideal of Enlightenment, to the Dharma as the fundamental spiritual principle discovered by him, together with their formulation in a body of teachings, and to the *Āryasangha* as the spiritual community of those who really follow those teachings.

In the context of the gāravas, however, the first of the Three Jewels is termed Satthā, which is yet another title accorded the Buddha, the full honorific usually being *satthā devamanussānaṁ*, 'teacher of gods and men'. Why the term Satthā appears here instead of 'Buddha' is probably because we experience the Buddha through the scriptures mainly as teacher – as supreme teacher, the teacher of gods and men. Also to be considered is the fact that in ancient India, as in almost all ages apart from our own, anyone who earned the title of 'teacher' automatically commanded great honour and reverence. It is still the case in India today – you call even your primary school teacher your 'guru' – and it is, of course, a term of great respect. In the Buddhist tradition, parents are often called 'the first gurus' – or to use another term with an equivalent meaning, 'the first *ācāryas*' – because they are the first people from whom you learn anything. And again, this represents a posture of respect. You respect your parents not only because they brought you into the world, but also because they were the first people from whom you learned anything.

The remaining three gāravas, after Satthā, Dharma, and Sangha, are less familiar. The fourth, *sikkhā*, is study, training, or discipline. Study is a gārava inasmuch as we cannot study Buddhism effectively unless we see it as something higher than we are, as having the power to help us to grow and develop, just as the rain and sunshine help plants and trees to grow. In Buddhism there are traditionally three objects of study or training: the higher ethics, the higher states of consciousness, and the higher wisdom. These are the pre-eminent sources from which we learn, grow, and develop. But there are all sorts of other things that benefit our human development – friendship and the fine arts, for example – and these too can be aspects of Buddhist study and training, and thus worthy of honour and respect. Thus the basic principle implied by the idea of study as a gārava is that if we are unable to honour and respect something, it isn't really worth studying, because it won't help us.

The fifth gārava is *appamāda*, or 'non-heedlessness' – that is, mindfulness or awareness. So why is mindfulness to be venerated? Why is it one of the six gāravas? The answer is quite simple. We have to respect those qualities that we are trying to develop. If we think rather lightly of them, if we don't really take them seriously, we won't get anywhere with them. In other words it behoves us to bring an attitude of reverence to our own spiritual practice, whether it be mindfulness or, indeed, any other discipline that we are taking up. *Appamāda* or non-heedlessness is named as the fifth gārava in an essentially representative sense, in the sense of being pivotal – the key – to all other Buddhist practice.

With the last of the gāravas we are introduced to a rather interesting word with a wide range of associated meanings: *paṭisanthāra*. It comes from a root meaning 'to spread', and its literal meaning is 'spreading before'. This probably leaves us none the wiser so far as identifying it as an object of respect is concerned. However, there is an English idiom that takes us a little closer to the nature of this gārava: 'laying out a good spread'. It is an old-fashioned expression, redolent of tuck-boxes and midnight feasts in the dormitory with one's chums – or high tea with an indulgent great-aunt – but you get the idea. A spread is a sort of feast, and *paṭisanthāra* has much the same kind of meaning. It means 'spreading before' in the sense of 'friendly welcome, kind reception, honour, goodwill, favour, friendship' – this is what the dictionary tells us. And the 'spreading before' can be material, or it can be spiritual. If you take it as meaning a 'kind reception' you can see that, as well as gastronomic feasting, it could suggest a feast, say, of music, and even 'the feast of reason and the flow of soul'.[16] At the highest level, it is a 'spreading' of spiritual abundance before people. Thus *paṭisanthāra* covers a rich, important aspect of human life, including spiritual life. And we will not be able to draw nourishment from it if we take it for granted. As well as honouring mindfulness, the heart of Buddhist practice, we also need to honour the whole expansive richness of the Buddhist life.

The significant place of reverence and worship in the spiritual life is made explicit in the teaching of the six gāravas. But as we have seen, it is clear from the evidence of the Buddha's own life, too, that worship is a spiritual requirement of every Buddhist, however highly developed. In fact, the greater the place we can give to worship in our own lives, the more certain we can be of one day attaining to whatever the Buddha himself attained, and of worshipping as the Buddha himself worshipped.

6

The Word of the Buddha

So the Buddha attained Enlightenment. He reached the end of his heroic quest. His aspiration was fulfilled. Then what? Enlightenment may have been in a sense the end of something, but it was also the start of something. It was the start of what we know as 'Buddhism', the emergence of the Dharma into the world. But in order for the Dharma, the Truth, to spread, the Buddha had to find a way of communicating his experience to other people. And, according to the traditional account of what transpired after his Enlightenment, the Buddha's decision to teach was not inevitable.

What he had realized seemed so tremendous, so overwhelming, that he began to wonder whether he could ever make it known to anybody else. Reality, in all its heights and all its depths, was so sublime, so unfathomable. It could never be reached through mere reasoning or dialectic. It was deep, delicate, and subtle. Only the truly wise would ever be able to understand it, because it went right against the grain of the world. And who had that kind of wisdom? Ordinary men and women were so absorbed in the pleasures of the senses that they couldn't take anything else seriously. What would be the point of trying to communicate his discovery to them? Even if he managed to speak to them on their own level, there would be nothing in their experience remotely like his own. How could he possibly get through to them?

The more he thought about it, the more inclined he was to hold his peace and leave the world to its own devices. But then, as he sat there under one of the trees at Buddha Gaya, enjoying the bliss of the Enlightenment experience, something happened to change his mind. In fact, according to the legends, it was some*one* who changed his mind. It was as if he saw a great light, heard a great voice; there appeared before him the great god Brahmā Sahampati. And the god spoke to him (we should note, by the way, that even he, lord of a thousand worlds, defers to the Buddha) saying, 'Let my Lord the Exalted One teach the Truth. For there are in the world at least a few people whose eyes are covered with but little of the dust of the passions. They will surely understand the Dharma, if you will only teach it to them.'[17]

That is what the scriptures say happened. Of course, as with so many events from the Buddha's life, you can take the incident either literally or symbolically. Either it happened more or less as described, or else the sublime figure of Brahmā Sahampati simply represents the level in the Buddha's mind at which this thought arose, a level that for all its sublimity was lower than that of Buddhahood itself. The voice, wherever it came from, was saying, 'Well, you've made it. You're Enlightened. You've reached your goal. You're at peace. You have perfect knowledge. You have perfect bliss. But what about the others? What about those who are still struggling? What are you going to do for *them*?' As the Buddha heard this voice, as he saw, as it were, this radiant figure in supplication before him, a great surge of compassion took place in his heart.

More prosaically, we may say that as the Buddha applied himself to the task of assimilating the Enlightenment experience at all levels of his being, one very important aspect of that assimilation process was the development of what we call – inadequately – *karuṇā*, or compassion. This, the compassion of a Buddha, is directed towards all those beings who are not Enlightened, who are suffering from their own ignorance, psychological conditioning, bewilderment, and confusion. So as he assimilated the Enlightenment experience in the deepest emotional aspect of his being, his ordinary human emotion was transformed into a transcendental quality of mind, into *karuṇā*.

Then with the supernormal power of his 'divine eye' the Buddha looked out over the world, and he perceived that the beings of the world were at widely differing stages of development. As he saw it, the world was, in this respect, like a muddy lake full of lotus plants. Some folk were deeply immersed in the world, like lotus buds buried deep in the mud. Others were not so completely engrossed in the world, and were beginning to emerge, like lotuses, from the muddy waters of the world. And there were a few who stood clear above those waters, ready to burst into bloom in the sunlight of the Truth.

Convinced at last that there were people in the world who would be receptive to the Truth, the Buddha addressed Brahmā Sahampati in verse. The English translation doesn't really capture the rhythm and beauty of the original Pali, but it is still very striking: 'Wide open are the gates leading to the deathless state. Let those that have ears to hear release their faith.'[18] So saying, he decided to go out into the world, and teach the truth he had discovered.

But having decided to teach, the next question was: whom should he teach? He cast his mind back to the earliest days of his going forth, and he thought of his first two teachers. They had not been able to show him the Truth themselves, but they had helped him as far as they could, and they were assuredly high-minded, noble individuals. If anyone could grasp what he had to teach, they could. But then the Buddha perceived that it was too late, that they were both dead. So then his thoughts turned to the five disciples who had followed him in the days when he was practising austerities. Although they had eventually left him in disgust, they had been very helpful to him for a time. Why not share his discovery with them first?

It is notable here that the Buddha is motivated in his initial attempts to teach not only by the fact that these particular individuals are ripe for the Dharma, but also by his gratitude towards them. It is interesting, in fact, that gratitude is clearly one of the keynotes of the Buddha's post-Enlightenment experience. Apparently, when he arose from the foot of the tree where he had actually become Enlightened, he walked some distance away from the tree, turned and looked at it for some hours together, and then saluted it. By this he was saying, in effect, 'This tree sheltered me, it shaded me while I gained Enlightenment. I pay respect and express gratitude to it.'

So it was in such a spirit of gratitude that the Buddha determined to find his five erstwhile followers. Perceiving in his mind where the five ascetics were, that they were living at a place called Sarnath, seven or eight miles out of Benares, the Buddha set out, leaving Buddha Gaya at the end of the seventh week after his Enlightenment.

Sarnath was about a hundred miles away – it must have taken a good week to get there – and he found the five ascetics living in the deer park, a sort of game sanctuary, also known as 'the resort of the seers'. They saw him coming, and recognized him while he was still some way off. They hadn't forgotten *him*. 'Here comes that fellow Gautama,' murmured one. 'You remember – we really thought he had it in him, until asceticism got too tough for him and he went back to the easy life. Look, you can see how strong and healthy he is, even from here.' Another said, 'Well, let him come if he wants to. He needn't think we're going to pay him any particular respect, though. We can't pay homage to the poor fellow as we used to when he was Gautama the great ascetic.' So the Buddha came nearer and nearer. And as he approached, the ascetics found themselves unable to keep to their resolution to ignore him. It was as though some strange force compelled them to rise to their feet, greet him, take his bowl and spare robe, and offer him a seat. Even though they disapproved of him – even though he had, as they thought, betrayed their common ideal – there was still something about him. It was something strange, something they'd never seen before, to which they could not help responding.

After the preliminary greetings were over, the Buddha came straight to the point: 'Listen. The Deathless has been attained. Let me teach you the way to reach this goal for yourselves.' But the five ascetics wouldn't believe him. They said, 'Even when you were practising all those austerities, even when you were mortifying the flesh with extremes of self-torture, you couldn't gain Enlightenment. How can you possibly have done it now, when everyone knows you've fallen by the wayside?' But the Buddha persisted. He reasoned with them, he argued with them, and in the end he managed to persuade them at least to listen to what he had to say. It was exactly two months from the date of his Enlightenment, and so it is this day, the full-moon day of June/July, which is celebrated as Dharmacakra-pravartana Day, that is, the anniversary of the Buddha's first turning of the Wheel of the Dharma. The rains had just begun, and throughout the months of the rainy season they talked, they debated, and they meditated. By the time the rain stopped, all five disciples had also gained Enlightenment.

Although the Buddha taught the five ascetics for all those months, it so happens that we simply don't know what it was that he taught. The oldest accounts simply say that he discoursed with them, and leave it at that. At a later date it was suggested that the Buddha taught the five ascetics the Four Noble Truths and the Noble Eightfold Path, but while he may well have done so we don't know for sure. Some people don't like anything unknown, so they prefer to fill in the blanks with something or other, and this is what seems to have happened here. What really took place remains a complete mystery, and perhaps it is best left that way.

Somehow or other, the Buddha had succeeded in communicating the ineffable, or rather, he had succeeded in leading his five disciples to their own direct experience of the ineffable truth of the Dharma. But this was only the start. For the next forty-five years he must have taught hundreds or even thousands of people, from all walks of life, up and down the length and breadth of north-eastern India, right up to the time of his death, or as we say, his *parinirvāṇa*, at the age of eighty. From the scriptures emerges a succession of countless unique occasions and encounters, each of which draws out a fresh insight into the Dharma:

• An important Brahmin comes to see the Buddha to ask him how best to conduct a great sacrifice of many hundreds of animals. Courteously and systematically, the Buddha convinces him that the most perfect sacrifice is a bloodless one, consisting in the practice of ethics, meditation, and Wisdom.

• A well-to-do farmer is busy organizing the sowing of his fields when he sees the Buddha standing there with his begging-bowl, and says to him, 'Why don't you try working for a living?' The Buddha gives a brilliant discourse, describing the spiritual life in terms of work. The farmer offers to reward him with a bowl of delicious food, but the Buddha refuses it; he is not to be hired or paid for his teaching.

• A number of monks overhear a wanderer speaking abusively of the Buddha and finding fault with the Dharma. The Buddha warns them not to get angry or upset on this account, nor to be pleased when people praise him and his teaching; but simply to acknowledge what is correct and explain what is incorrect in the views of others.

• One of the Buddha's lay-followers suggests that the local people would take to the Dharma much more readily if the monks could be persuaded to perform superhuman feats and miracles. The Buddha explains that the only miracle that is of any real use is the miracle of instruction in the Dharma which brings an end to suffering.

• Two novice monks from Brahmin backgrounds admit to the Buddha that Brahmins have been reviling and abusing them for renouncing their caste in order to join the Sangha. The Buddha reassures them: there is no real distinction to be drawn between members of different castes, either physical, moral, or spiritual; but anyone whose faith is unshakeable becomes a true son and heir of the Buddha and the Dharma.

• A king is inspired by the beauty of a moonlit night to go with his retinue to seek peace of mind from the Buddha....

• A monk comes with the news that a raucous and intemperate dispute has broken out among the Order....

• A great crowd is gathered to listen to a discourse, and the Buddha sees that there is only one among them, a leper, who is really going to hear what he has to say....

• An old woman, distraught with grief at the death of her granddaughter, comes to the Buddha for comfort....

In this way people kept coming and the Buddha responded to them according to their individual spiritual needs. Some went away as ignorant as they came, others went away with some food for thought, but for many, their lives would never be the same again. They would marvel aloud: 'It is as if someone were to set up what had been knocked down, or to point out the way to one who had got lost, or to bring an oil lamp into a dark place.... I go for Refuge to the Dharma and the Sangha.' And then they would ask to be accepted as a lay-follower or ordained as a monk or nun.

The Buddha's last disciple was someone who came to see him when he was literally on his deathbed. Ānanda, the Buddha's disciple and attendant, was all for sending this person (his name was Subhadda) away. The Buddha was dying. This was hardly the time to ask him for yet another teaching. But the Buddha overheard their talk and said to Ānanda, 'Let him in. Whatever he wants to ask is for the sake of knowledge, not to cause trouble. What I tell him he will quickly understand.' So in he came, the last person to be personally instructed by the Buddha.

After the Buddha had passed away, his disciples carried on the teaching, passing it on to their own pupils, who then, in time, passed it on to theirs. They passed it on, of course, by word of mouth. People didn't start scribbling books about Buddhism, or even taking notes. In fact, the teachings were not written down in any form for hundreds of years. If you wanted to learn about Buddhism, you had to find someone at whose feet you could sit and learn about it. People only started to write down the Buddha's teaching about 500 years after his death, perhaps because by that time people's memories weren't as good as they had been in earlier days, and there was a danger that the Dharma would be lost.

The teaching that the Buddha taught personally to his disciples, and which was transmitted orally for so many years before eventually being written down in the form of scriptures, is known as *Buddhavacana*. 'Buddha' is a title meaning 'One who knows', while *vacana* means 'word' or 'utterance' or 'speech'. So Buddhavacana is the word, the utterance, the speech, of one who really does know. It is no ordinary speech. It is quite unlike the speech of anybody who is not a Buddha. This is because Buddhavacana is the expression in terms of human speech of an Enlightened state of consciousness.

There is always more to this than one can imagine. We tend to assume, perhaps unconsciously, that the Buddha speaks in much the same way that an ordinary person does, because, after all, he uses much the same language as everybody around him. But behind the common mode of communication there is something in the Buddha's speech that is not there behind our own speech. Informing the Buddha's words, standing behind them, as it were, there is the Enlightened consciousness, the Buddha-mind. And 'for those who have ears to hear', the words of the Buddha express that Buddha-mind. However, those words cannot be said to express the Buddha-mind directly. In fact, although words are the most obvious medium of communication, they provide only one of the ways – perhaps the least direct way – in which the Buddha expresses Enlightenment. Between the Enlightened state of consciousness and its expression in terms of ordinary human speech there are several inter-mediate levels of communication, and these levels are also implicit in our use of the term Buddhavacana. They represent the deeper – or at least some of the deeper – implications of the term.

First of all there is the level – if we can call it that, because it is a level beyond all levels – of the Enlightened mind, the Buddha-mind itself. We use this expression 'Buddha-mind', but actually it is very difficult for us to get any idea of what the Buddha-mind is like, because in it there is no subject and no object. All that we can say about it – and even this is misleading – is that it is pure, undifferentiated awareness, abso-lutely void, absolutely luminous. It is one continuous 'mass' of spiritual luminosity. If this manner of speaking leaves us none the wiser, we can take a different approach. We can say that this level of experience is completely, deeply, ultimately, absolutely, satisfying, that it comprises peace and bliss beyond all human understanding. Another way of putting it would be to say that the Buddha-mind is above and beyond space and time. Or, to put it yet another way, at that level of experience everything is known because in it there is nothing to be known.

So is that clear? Well, no. We can hardly express in words what is by definition utterly beyond them. The consciousness of a Buddha is inconceivable to us in our ordinary state of consciousness, dominated as it is by the subject–object distinction. Perhaps the nearest we can get to it is through metaphor, by describing the Buddha-mind as a vast and shoreless ocean in which millions of universes are just one tiny wave – or even just a fleck of foam – in the midst of that boundless ocean.

So now we have to try to conceive of there arising, within this inconceivable Enlightened mind, the desire to communicate. Again, this is not strictly conceivable, because we have to speak in terms of time ('arising') and space ('within'), even though the Enlightened mind transcends space and time. Nor is it truly feasible to use the word 'desire' of a mind that is totally at peace. However, as we have already recounted, the desire to communicate in some sense did arise within the Enlightened mind of the Buddha. And what the Enlightened mind desires to communicate is, of course, itself. It can hardly communicate anything else. In fact, we may say that the Enlightened mind is an Enlightenment-communicating mind. And this desire on the part of the Enlightened consciousness to communicate with the non-Enlightened consciousness, on whatever level the non-Enlightened consciousness is found, is what we call compassion.

This communication at the highest level is very, very subtle. There is nothing obvious about it at all. It's like a sort of tremor, a sort of vibration, that passes between the Enlightened mind and the mind that is just a little short of Enlightenment. Speaking quite metaphorically, this tremor or vibration you may say is *like* an extremely subtle sound. It is not sound in the ordinary sense, not gross external sound of the kind you can hear with your physical ears, or even sound you can hear inside your own head. It is a kind of primordial sound, something on the spiritual plane which corresponds to what we know as sound. This tremor, this vibration, this soundless sound, is the Buddhavacana in the highest sense of the term. This is the sound emitted, as it were, by the Buddha-mind – even by Reality itself. And because the Buddha-mind is not limited by time or confined by space, there is no moment or place where it does not give out this vibration.

Some Indian traditions identify this primordial, cosmic sound with the mantra *oṁ*. This is not a syllable pronounced by any human tongue. It is a subtle, inner, spiritual sound which can sometimes be heard in higher states of consciousness such as those attained in meditation. If you are attuned to it, you can hear it coming from all things, all phenomena of the universe, because the Buddha-mind is as it were behind them all, even within them all, and shines through them, sounds through them.

When you hear this sound, you hear in its most subtle form the word of the Buddha. Hearing it, you hear that everything is in this sound, and you understand everything. No words are necessary. No thoughts are necessary. There isn't any need for images. There's just this one primordial, undifferentiated vibration sounding forth from the Buddha-mind, the Buddha-consciousness, from Reality. You hear all, understand all, realize all, just from this sound *oṁ* coming from everything, everywhere, all the time. This is Buddhavacana in the highest sense, on the highest level.

As we can imagine, this level of communication is almost unimaginably lofty, so the Enlightened mind has to come down, so to speak, step by step, to relatively lower levels of communication. And the next step down is the level of archetypal images: images of the sun and the moon and the stars, images of light and darkness, images of the heavens and the earth, images of birds and beasts and flowers, images of rain and wind and thunder and lightning; images of Buddhas and Bodhisattvas, images of gods and goddesses, images benign and wrathful, images of all sorts of monstrous shapes; perhaps above all, images brilliantly coloured, shining, luminous.

These images are not created by the individual human mind, nor even, perhaps, by the 'collective unconscious'. Indeed, they are perhaps not created at all, but coeval, co-eternal, with the Enlightened consciousness itself – at least, so far as this particular level of communication is concerned. They arise out of the depths of infinite space, and like the primordial sound, they reveal everything, tell everything. They image forth the Buddha-mind throughout the universe in terms of form and colour. Here in the world of images, no thoughts are necessary, no ideas, no words are necessary. Communication is not so subtle as it is at the level of mantric sound, but it is still far subtler and far more comprehensive than anything we ordinarily experience.

Coming down one step further, the Enlightened mind also expresses itself on the level of conceptual thought. Conceptual thought is common to both the Enlightened and the unenlightened mind, in that it is created by the unenlightened mind, but it can be used, taken over, even transformed, by the Enlightened mind in accordance with its own higher purpose. This is what essentially distinguishes what is sometimes called Buddhist philosophy or Buddhist thought from what we normally think of as philosophical thought. 'Buddhist thought' does not consist of the speculations of ordinary, unenlightened Buddhists. Doctrines like conditioned co-production are not intellectual theories. In the true sense, Buddhist thought is a series of attempts on the part of the Enlightened mind – whether that of Gautama the Buddha or that of other Enlightened beings – to communicate with unenlightened minds through the medium of concepts.

It may come as a surprise to find that below the conceptual level comes that of words, the lowest level at which the Enlightened mind communicates. Some people would say that it is not really possible to separate words and thoughts. Certainly the connection between the two is very close, closer than that between thoughts and images. Nevertheless, thoughts and words are not quite the same thing. We do sometimes have thoughts which we do not, or cannot, put into words.

We can now see the enormous gulf that separates the Enlightened mind from its expression in terms of ordinary human speech. We can see through how many levels the Buddha had to descend, as it were, before he could communicate himself to the five ascetics. No wonder it took him eight weeks to make the transition. We can think of this as 'coming down' in a way, but it is not that he left the previous levels behind. It is more like an extension of his range of communication. So Buddhavacana, the word of the Buddha, consists of all these levels of communication – primordial mantric sound, archetypal images, concepts, and words – and on all these levels the Dharma, the Buddha's teaching, is transmitted. The Dharma as the Buddha's teaching is not just a matter of words and concepts.

The Tantric tradition of India and Tibet explicitly acknowledges this point, that Buddhavacana is more than just words. It emphasizes it in a rather different way, but with much the same meaning. What it does is identify three modes of transmission of the Dharma. First of all there is what the Tantra calls the mind transmission of the Jinas, or 'Conquerors'. Here the transmission takes place from mind to mind, from heart to heart, from consciousness to consciousness. There are no words. There is no thought. The communication flashes directly, intuitively, telepathically, from one mind to another. The Buddha looks at you, as it were, and you know it. That's the end of the matter. Neither of you says anything, neither of you thinks anything. The transmission takes place on a purely mental or even spiritual level.

The second mode of transmission is the transmission of the *vidyā-dharas*. The *vidyādharas* are the great Tantric initiates, the Tantric masters. They are not fully Enlightened, like the Jinas, but by ordinary human standards they are inconceivably developed, spiritually. On this level the transmission is through actions and gestures. In the Ch'an tradition of China a famous story is told of the Buddha's silent sermon. He simply holds up a golden flower. He says nothing, he just holds up a flower, and somebody understands. The gesture is lost on the rest of the audience, who are all ears, waiting for the Buddha to say something profound. But for one of them, Kaśyapa, it is enough, this simple gesture. There are some Tantric initiations, even today, in which the master just points. He doesn't say anything, doesn't explain anything. He just points, and that's that. If the disciple is receptive enough, he gets what has been literally pointed out. There are no words, there is no discussion, but if you're really alert, you get the point, there and then.

Thirdly and lastly, right at the bottom of the list, there is the transmission through words by the *ācāryas*. The *ācāryas* are ordinary teachers of Buddhism, people who are not fully Enlightened, but have some measure of insight, and faithfully hand on the teaching through the medium of ordinary human thought and speech.

All these are valid transmissions. You can get the spirit of the Dharma, the heart of the Dharma, through telepathy, through signs and gestures, and through words, but, of course, the lower the level of transmission, the greater the possibility of misunderstanding. If the communication flashes directly from mind to mind there is no question of misunderstanding, because there is no question even of understanding – and if there's no understanding, how can there be misunderstanding? With a gesture there is a little scope for confusion, because you may not quite see what is being pointed at; you may see something a bit different. On the level of words, however, the chances of misunderstanding are very great indeed.

The first safeguard against misunderstanding the Dharma as expressed in words is to ensure that both the letter and the spirit of the teachings are faithfully recorded. For many years this was the responsibility of the monks who memorized the teachings and passed them down through the generations by word of mouth. Even when people did start to write things down, it was a very gradual process – so gradual, in fact, that apparently some things were never written down at all, and are still being transmitted by word of mouth right down to the present day.

As soon as an oral teaching is committed to writing, it becomes a 'sacred scripture', and these sacred scriptures, the literary records of what were originally oral teachings, are known as the word of the Buddha, Buddhavacana. In fact, the term 'word of the Buddha' is often used almost exclusively in the sense of the scriptures, and its deeper implications rather forgotten. But although they are only one aspect of Buddhavacana, it is important to have an awareness of the canon of Buddhist literature – which has, over the centuries, grown very large indeed. We will consider the scriptures in their main categories, roughly in the order in which they appeared as literary documents – which is over a period of nearly a thousand years. Broadly speaking, the more exoteric teachings seem to have been written down first, while the more esoteric ones were recorded later on, or perhaps even not at all.

The first category of teachings to be written down is certainly the most exoteric. This is the monastic code, the Vinaya, which consists essentially of rules of conduct for monks and nuns. The rules of the Vinaya are of two kinds. There are rules for those monks and nuns leading a wandering life and living off alms: these rules are known as the *bhikṣu prātimokṣa* and the *bhikṣuṇī prātimokṣa*. And there are rules known as the *skandhakas* or 'chapters' for monks and nuns living in permanently residential communities. The chapters cover all sorts of subjects. There's a chapter on ordination, a chapter on the fortnightly gatherings of the wanderers, and a chapter on how to observe the rainy season retreat. There are rules about medicine, food, and material for robes; there are sleeping regulations and rules for sick monks. There are rules about dwellings and furnishings – they seem to have acquired furnishings rather quickly – and there's even a chapter on the use of leather for shoes. Other rules cover the order of precedence among monks, how to settle disputes and schisms, and the duties of monks under suspension. All these disparate topics, and lots more, are covered.

The Vinaya does not just consist of a list of rules. It also includes commentaries on the rules, that is, explanations of them, plus historical, biographical, and anthropological material. Altogether it comprises a bulky corpus of teachings and information. In fact, the Vinaya literature is probably our richest source of information about the general condition of north-eastern India in the Buddha's time. You also find, dotted here and there, quite a few discourses. As far as modern scholars can discern, some of the material in the Vinaya – and this includes some of the rules – cannot be counted as literally the actual word of the Buddha, but was added later by disciples. This later incorporation of extra material is not unique to the Vinaya, incidentally, but applies to practically all branches of the scriptures.

The second category of scriptures consists of the dialogues and discourses of the Buddha. There are about 200 of these, some long and some short, and most of them are arranged in two great collections: the 'Long Discourses' and the 'Middle-Length Discourses'. In the Pali recension, there are 34 long discourses and 152 middle-length ones. Between them, they cover all aspects of moral and spiritual life. Some are of anthropological interest, some of mythological interest, and some even of autobiographical interest, because in them the Buddha recounts the experiences of his own earlier life. It's a rich and rather miscellaneous collection.

Thirdly, there are the 'anthologies' – anthologies of sayings of the Buddha, of which the most famous is the *Dhammapada*. This Buddhist classic is quite short, but there are two particularly large anthologies, containing between them thousands of sayings, all systematically arranged. One of them is arranged according to subject matter, bringing under one heading all the Buddha's sayings on a particular topic. There's a collection of sayings on the gods, one on Māra the Evil One, one on Vaṅgīsa, who was one of the Buddha's most gifted disciples and a fine poet, and one on Maudgalyāyana, another of the Buddha's disciples, famous for his psychic powers. There are sayings on nuns, sayings on Brahmins, sayings on the heavenly musicians, plus others on Stream Entry, on views, on the defilements, and on the Four Foundations of Mindfulness.

Another anthology arranges sayings numerically. For instance, in the section on 'the fours' you get the four things leading to liberation from conditioned existence, the four kinds of purity of a gift, the four kinds of thoroughbred (thoroughbred horses, apparently), the four *dhyānas* (states of higher consciousness), the four *brahma vihāras* (love, compassion, joy, and equanimity), and so on. Similarly, you get 'the ones', 'the twos', and so on up to 'the elevens'. The arrangement would clearly have been a useful mnemonic device in the days of oral transmission.

The fourth category is that of the Jātakas, or 'Birth Stories', and the Avadānas, or 'Glorious Deeds'. These are perhaps the most widely popular of all Buddhist scriptures. They are especially loved by the lay people in all traditional Buddhist countries, from Sri Lanka to Tibet. And this is not surprising, since they consist entirely of stories, many of which are enthralling enough to stand up well just as stories. The Jātakas are all about the Buddha, while the Avadānas recount fables relating to his closest disciples. But they are stories with a difference, in that they concern the *previous* lives of these various individuals. They effectively illustrate the workings of the law of karma, the law of moral and psychological recompense over a whole series of lifetimes, showing how one's moral and spiritual gains are conserved, as it were, from one life to the next.

The Jātakas are much more numerous than the Avadānas, and the biggest collection of Jātakas, 550 of them – some the length of short novels – is in Pali. Most of the stories follow a standard pattern of four parts. An introduction describes the particular occasion on which the Buddha is supposed to have narrated this particular Jātaka story to his disciples. Then there's the Jātaka story proper. Thirdly, there are some verses which generally follow on from the prose story. Lastly, the Buddha identifies the characters in the story; he says, for instance, 'Well, Ānanda, you were so-and-so in the story, and I was so-and-so – and Devadatta was so-and-so.' Sometimes the stories aren't very complimentary even to the Buddha himself. He is certainly no saint in some of his past lives, and in one story he is even a robber, which shows there's hope for everybody.

Many Jātaka stories are old Indian folk tales, taken over by the Buddhists and adapted to their own particular purposes. T. W. Rhys Davids has gone so far as to describe the Pali Jātaka book as the most reliable, the most complete, and the most ancient collection of folklore now extant in any literature in the world. What is beyond doubt is that the Jātakas and the Avadānas have exerted an enormous moral and spiritual influence in the Buddhist East. Right down to recent times dramatic versions of them were staged on special occasions in the courtyards of the big monasteries of Tibet – probably the most effective way of moving and inspiring Tibetan herdsmen, traders, and mule-drivers with the word of the Buddha.

Our fifth category is something very different. In the Abhidharma there are no stories at all, and even figures of speech are utterly banished. The purpose of this literature is the definition of technical terms (which is much more important, when you think about it, than it sounds) and the analysis and classification of mental states. It attempts also to give a complete systematic account, mainly in psychological terms, of the whole path to nirvāṇa. So the task the compilers of the Abhidharma set themselves was to gather together the teachings found in the dialogues, discourses, and anthologies, and to analyse them. All personal references were edited out. History, biography, mythology, poetry, and rhetoric were eliminated. Their results still make a good shelf-full, though. The word Abhidharma is usually explained as the 'higher' or 'further' teaching of the Buddha. Some schools take the view, however, that while there are some traces of the Abhidharma method in the dialogues and anthologies, the Abhidharma itself should be treated, not as the literal word of the Buddha, but as the product of later scholastic activity.

According to the schools of the so-called Hīnayāna tradition, the 'Lesser Way', this is as far as the word of the Buddha can be said to go. At this point we leave behind the Pali canon and move on to scriptures that are accepted as canonical only by the Mahāyāna tradition. However, the Mahāyāna sūtras, the sixth category, form one of the largest and richest divisions of the Buddhist scriptures. They deal, of course, primarily with specifically Mahāyāna teachings – śūnyatā (the voidness), the Bodhisattva ideal, the One Mind, the Trikāya (the three bodies of a Buddha) and so on. But they are also called 'sūtras' and are thus records of discourses given by the Buddha. Out of several hundred Mahāyāna sūtras, some are very long indeed, consisting of several volumes, while others run to only a page or two. Some of them are written in a quiet, philosophical style, while others are full of myth and symbolism, marvels and magic.

A brief résumé can hardly do justice to the Mahāyāna sūtras – all we can do is mention a few of the most famous ones. First, there's *The Perfection of Wisdom in 8,000 Lines*. This is one of the oldest texts from the Perfection of Wisdom tradition, dealing mainly with *Prajñāpāramitā*, 'the wisdom that goes beyond'. It deals also with the person who strives to develop this Perfect Wisdom, the Bodhisattva, and with the focus of Perfect Wisdom – śūnyatā, the Void, unfathomable Reality. Making relentless use of paradox, the text stresses again and again the subtle, elusive, trans-conceptual nature of this wisdom.

Next, a totally different Mahāyāna sūtra. From a literary point of view the *Saddharma Puṇḍarīka*, the 'White Lotus of the Real Truth', is one of the most marvellous, impressive, and magnificent of them all. It conveys a profound spiritual meaning, but it conveys it for the most part in entirely non-conceptual terms. It contains no abstract teaching, no philosophy, no conceptual statements. Instead, it is full of parables, myths, and symbols, and through these it expresses two great teachings: that in essence the Buddha is eternal, above and beyond space and time; and that there is just one great way to Enlightenment for all beings – the Mahāyāna. According to the *White Lotus Sūtra* all living beings, whether they know it or not, are following this path, and will in the end gain Enlightenment. It thus emphasizes the spiritual optimism of the Buddhist vision at the highest possible level.

The *Laṅkāvatāra Sūtra* is said to have been expounded by the Buddha in the course of a visit to the mythical island of Laṅka (not to be confused with the modern Sri Lanka). It teaches, among other things, that the whole of conditioned existence is ultimately nothing but one mind, one absolute and ultimate consciousness to which everything can be reduced, and of which everything, in one way or another, is the manifestation. The emphasis in this text is on the need actually to realize this. It is not enough just to talk about it, or just to think about it, or even just to meditate upon it. One needs to realize for oneself, within oneself, that everything is just mind. What the *Laṅkāvatāra* then also stresses is that in order to do this one needs to undergo a radical transformation. One's whole mental apparatus, one's whole psychological system, must be put into reverse, turned upside-down, transformed. This transformation the *Laṅkāvatāra Sūtra* calls the *parāvṛtti*, the 'turning about in the deepest seat of consciousness', a turning about from the split, fractured mind to the One Mind. This is the ultimate message of the *Laṅkāvatāra Sūtra*.

The vision of the universe we get in the *Gaṇḍavyūha Sūtra* is different again. It gives an account of a young pilgrim called Sudhana, a seeker after truth. In the course of his pilgrimage, all over India and beyond, he visits more than fifty teachers, and they are of many kinds. They include Bodhisattvas, monks, nuns, and householders; there's a physician, a sailor, a perfume seller, two kings, several children, a number of deities, and also a hermit; and Sudhana learns something from each and every one of them. Eventually, at the end of his long journey, he comes to the Vairocana Tower in southern India. There he meets the Bodhisattva Maitreya and receives his final 'initiation'. Within the tower he has a vision of the Absolute Truth. Mysteriously able to see the whole cosmos and everything in it, he perceives that everything in the cosmos reflects everything else, that everything in the universe interpenetrates with everything else like mutually intersecting beams of light. He sees that things are not separate, demarcated, solid, but fluid and flowing; every thing flows into every other thing, all the time, everywhere.

The sūtra upon which Edwin Arnold based his famous poem, *The Light of Asia*, is the *Lalitavistara*, which means 'the extended account of the sports'. This might seem like an odd title for a biography of the

Buddha, even a highly imaginative and poetic biography, as this one is. But it emphasizes an important aspect of the Buddha's nature, because the word 'sports' is meant to indicate the playful spontaneity of the Buddha's actions. After his Enlightenment there was no question of being conditioned, or determined by anything, or being subject to karma. It was all free, creative, playful manifestation of his Enlightened essence. And this is what the title *Lalitavistara* is getting at.

This is no more than a glimpse of a few of the very many sūtras of the Mahāyāna – even a catalogue of their titles would take over this book. It is even more difficult, however, to offer an adequate account of the seventh and last branch of the Buddhist scriptures, the Tantras. They are not systematic treatises or discourses. They are written – though this word makes them sound more like literary compositions than they really are – in a cryptic, even deliberately misleading way. You're not meant to be able to read a Tantra and understand it – as will be obvious if you manage to get hold of a Tantric text. You're not supposed to read, let alone practise the content of, the Tantra at all without initiation by a guru. The guru takes from the Tantras what he thinks you need, organizes it to suit your personal practice, and initiates you accordingly. That is all one can usefully say about this particular branch of Buddhist literature.

These seven categories of the Buddhist scriptures – the monastic code, the dialogues and discourses, the anthologies, the birth stories and heroic deeds, the Abhidharma, the Mahāyāna sūtras, and the Tantras – constitute between them the Buddhavacana, the word of the Buddha, in its most external and exoteric sense. Altogether, these literary records of oral teachings amount to a small library. At present they exist in three main collections: the Pali Tipitāka, the Chinese San Tsang, and the Tibetan Kangyur. The Pali Tipiṭaka is the scriptural basis of the Buddhism of south-east Asia – mainly Sri Lanka, Thailand, and Burma – and it is of course in the Pali language, which is based on an old Indian dialect. It contains versions of the first five categories of scriptures – practically all of it by now translated into English – but nothing else. The Chinese San Tsang is even more voluminous than the Pali Tipiṭaka, and it contains versions of all the categories of scriptures except the Tantras (although one or two Tantras are included in early sūtra form). It consists of translations into Chinese, mainly from Sanskrit. And the Kangyur, which consists of translations into Tibetan from Sanskrit, is in a sense the most complete collection of Buddhist scriptures, because it contains all seven categories. However, very little of either of these collections has been translated into English.

It is very easy to get lost among all these Buddhist scriptures, even among the English translations, comparatively few as they are. It is very easy to get confused about what to read and what not to read. It is even easy to forget what the word of the Buddha is in a deeper sense. Among all the words we can lose the Word itself. Reading and studying so many scriptures, it is so easy to forget the spirit of the Buddhavacana. Under these circumstances we need a teacher to help interpret all these texts, to elucidate a clear path for us as individuals to follow. On our own we will see a multiplicity of teachings before us, some of which are appropriate to where we are now and some of which are not. We need someone with greater experience than we have, who can help us through difficult patches and suggest where we might change the emphasis of our practice or change direction altogether. Otherwise we can lose heart, or even lose ourselves up blind alleys. No one, not even the Buddha, has ever been incapable of making mistakes, and these can sometimes be big mistakes.

Above all, we need our spiritual friends, that is, friends who relate to us on the basis of a common spiritual commitment to a common spiritual ideal. In our communication with those who relate to us on the basis of what is best and highest in us, we can turn the theory of the Dharma into practice. It is only in relation to other people that we can really gauge the effectiveness of our own spiritual practice, and it is those who know us at our best as well as at our worst who can provide the most helpful and precise advice with it. So important and delightful is the communication with spiritual friends to anyone who has experienced it that the Buddha's attendant Ānanda was once moved to suggest that 'spiritual friendship is half the spiritual life'. The Buddha replied, 'Say not so, Ānanda. Spiritual friendship is the *whole* of the spiritual life.'[19] Indeed, Enlightenment itself, inasmuch as it communicates itself, exemplifies spiritual friendship at the highest level, most notably in the Buddha's relationship with Ānanda. Despite their inequality in spiritual attainment, they looked after each other with mutual kindness for the last twenty years of the Buddha's life.

The Buddhavacana can only come alive in the context of the Sangha. Otherwise it remains a dead letter. This is why the integrity and harmony of the Order of monks was the Buddha's first concern. If his followers lived in concord, with open and clear communication with one another, and with friendliness and care for each other's welfare, the spirit of the Buddhavacana would be preserved.

However, there is more to the Sangha than meets the eye. We can also connect with the spirit of the Buddhavacana by leaving behind, for a moment, the world we are familiar with, and approaching instead a different realm, that of archetypal images. There we will find that the Buddhavacana appears embodied in the figure of the Bodhisattva Mañjughoṣa, the Bodhisattva of Wisdom. His name means 'he of gentle speech', and he is also known as Vagīśvara, which means 'Lord of Speech' (the root of this name, *vag*, is also, by the way, the root of *vacana*). Vagīśvara, sovereign of speech, appears in the midst of the dark blue, midnight sky in the form of a beautiful youth, sixteen years of age, and tawny – a rich yellow – in colour. Seated cross-legged on a lotus, he is clad in silks and jewels, and has long, black, flowing hair. In one hand he wields a sword streaming fire, and in the other he holds a book which he presses to his heart, a book which contains the scriptures, or more particularly, the Perfection of Wisdom scriptures. He is surrounded by an aura of golden light, which is in turn surrounded by rainbows. This is Mañjughoṣa, Vagīśvara, Lord of Speech, and he is the embodiment, the archetype, of the word of the Buddha.

We can go even further, even higher, than that. The word of the Buddha is embodied not only in the figure of a Bodhisattva, but in the figure of the Buddha himself, the Buddha of the *White Lotus Sūtra*. In that sūtra we are told that the Buddha is seated eternally on the spiritual Vulture's Peak, the very summit of mundane existence. There he eternally proclaims the Dharma – but he does not proclaim it in words as written down in the text of the sūtra, nor even in images as described in the text of the sūtra. He proclaims it in terms of pure mantric sound, as the primordial vibration, so to speak, of Reality itself. Whether we are meditating or reading the scriptures, whenever we are silent and still, we can pick up that vibration, coming, as it were, from the Buddha-mind, on the farthest pinnacle of existence. As we pick it up we can ourselves begin to vibrate very subtly in accordance with it, in harmony with it. We too can hear in that way, to that extent, in the very depths, in the very heights, of our being. In the deepest, highest, truest, most comprehensive sense, we can hear the word of the Buddha.

7

KARMA AND REBIRTH

OLD AGE, SICKNESS, AND DEATH were the spurs to Siddhārtha Gautama's quest, and what he realized when he became the Buddha somehow put an end to these things. It was not just that he came to terms with death, it was not even that he looked forward to death. He realized something – not intellectually but by way of direct perception – that transformed him into a new species of being to whom birth and death simply did not apply. As we have seen in the previous chapter, the Buddha doubted at first the possibility of communicating this alchemical insight – what he called 'the truth of *pratītya-samutpāda*' – to anyone else. But communicate it he did, deep and subtle as it was. And though his seminal formulation of *pratītya-samutpāda* engendered, over the years, a vast and rich array of teachings, it remains the basis, the very foundation, of all of them. In philosophical terms, at least, it is the realization of this truth of universal conditionality which constitutes the essence of the Buddha's Enlightenment. Hence we describe it as the fundamental principle of Buddhism.

It originally took the form in his mind of a laconic, even bleak statement: 'This is conditioned by that. All that happens is by way of a cause.' However, the most renowned version of this principle derives, perhaps significantly, from an occasion when it was being *communicated*

– and with dramatic success. In this particular instance it was in fact communicated not by the Buddha himself, but by one of his disciples, and it was imparted to a seeker after the truth who was to become the Buddha's chief disciple.

It was a few months after the Buddha's Enlightenment. A young Brahmin from Bihar called Śāriputra had gone forth from home, just as the Buddha had, along with his childhood friend Maudgalyāyana. He was now on his own because the two of them had agreed that they would go off in different directions, and that whichever of them found an Enlightened teacher first would tell the other, thus doubling their chances, so to speak.

In the course of his travels, Śāriputra happened to meet one of the Buddha's first five disciples, called Aśvajit, who had by this time become Enlightened himself and gone forth to teach the Dharma. Very much impressed by the appearance of this wandering monk, who radiated tranquillity and happiness, Śāriputra approached him, greeted him, and asked 'Who is your teacher?' This might seem to us a rather direct way of addressing a total stranger. In Britain we generally open a conversation with a remark like 'Nice weather we're having,' or 'Looks like it's beginning to clear up a bit now.' But in India they tend to come straight to the point. So Śāriputra asked the question that people in India still ask each other when they meet in this way, and Aśvajit answered, 'My teacher is Śākyamuni, the Sage, the Wise One of the Śākya tribe, the Buddha.' Śāriputra then put to Aśvajit the second standard question – standard, but in this case, anyway, also momentous: 'What does he teach?' Aśvajit said, 'Frankly, I'm a beginner. I really don't know much about the Dharma. But I can tell you in brief what it's about.' And what he then said has since become famous throughout the Buddhist world in the form of a short Pali verse of just two lines. He said, or pronounced – or perhaps even declaimed:

Of all those things that proceed from a cause, the Tathāgata[20] has explained the cause, and also its cessation. This is the teaching of the great *śramaṇa*.'[21]

It seems that this stanza made a shattering, and at the same time liberating, impression on the mind of Śāriputra. He had an instantaneous glimpse of the truth that it embodied. Transcendental insight arose in him, and he became a Stream Entrant on the spot. Obviously, the ground had been so well prepared that this most compressed exposition of the Dharma was enough to tell him his quest was at an end. He could go to his friend, Maudgalyāyana, and tell him with confidence that he had found the Buddha.

You will find this verse of Aśvajit's recorded, honoured, and worshipped all over the Eastern Buddhist world. In Tibet, China, Japan, Thailand, Sri Lanka, it is found carved on stone monuments and clay tablets, printed on strips of paper to be stuffed inside images, and inscribed on plates of silver or gold. It is, we may say, the credo of Buddhism. If it seems rather dry and abstract, academic, uninspiring even, it certainly did not seem so to Śāriputra. And when you really think about the principle of *pratītya-samutpāda* – in whatever form it is put – when you meditate on it, when you really follow through its implications, you begin to understand the extraordinary impact it has had on the world. Whatever comes into existence on whatever level, does so in dependence on conditions, and in the absence of those conditions it ceases to exist. This is all it says. But if anything is Buddhism, this is Buddhism.

What it is saying is that, from the viewpoint of the Enlightened mind, the outstanding feature of all phenomena, whether physical or psychical, is that they are conditioned. The unceasing flux of things, both material events and states of mind, is a process of interdependent stages, each of which comes about through the presence of conditions and, in its turn, conditions the stages succeeding it. Rainfall, sunshine, and the nourishing earth are the conditions from which arises the oak tree, whose fallen leaves rot and form the rich humus from which the bluebell grows. A jealous attachment will have consequences that may lead to murder. Nothing phenomenal is spontaneously produced without preceding conditions, or itself fails to have consequences. And it is the process of becoming aware of this law of conditionality that gradually liberates us from all conditions, leading to the freely functioning, spontaneous creativity of Enlightenment.

If we are reasonably clear about what it was that constituted the Buddha's realization, we can move on to look at how it actually dealt with the questions that Siddhārtha originally set out to answer. What about old age, sickness, and death? Where do the immutable facts of our physical decay fit into the whole process of conditionality? Does this 'unceasing flux of things' continue beyond death – or is death the end? These questions, of course, are not abstract or theoretical for us. The mystery of death which so troubled primitive humanity is still a mystery. Even these days, when we apparently know so much, you only need to give a talk called 'The Tibetan Book of the Dead' or 'What happens after death' or 'Where you go when you die' to draw record crowds. And there is always a healthy market for books about death and dying. We may think things have changed immeasurably since primitive times, but they haven't changed much when it comes to our understanding of death. Indeed, if anything, the 'problem' of death has become more pressing.

We are not, however, talking here about one single problem of death common to everyone. The way we feel about death, and the way we come to terms – or not – with death, is not exactly the same as the way other people feel about it. And people's feelings and ideas about death have changed over time, over the centuries, as well. Putting the problem of death into some kind of historical perspective, we may say that it all really began when mankind first started growing crops, in the age of the great river valley civilizations. This was perhaps ten or fifteen thousand years ago. At that time the world began to take on an aspect that was less hostile and mysterious, but people were still in the dark about the greatest of all mysteries – death. The mystery, in fact, grew deeper and darker, and it seemed to weigh on people's minds more oppressively than ever before. And there was a reason for this. People no longer wandered about in roving bands; they lived in villages and towns, even in great cities. Civilization as we know it, so to speak, had begun. Life had become more secure and comfortable, and people enjoyed it more. And having begun to enjoy it, they wanted to go on enjoying it. They didn't want to leave their wives or husbands, their children, their houses and their neatly cultivated fields, their singing and their dancing, their games of chance and their religious rites – but one day they would have to, and they knew it. The thought of death threw a shadow over the sunlight of their lives. What was life for, if it had to end so soon? You had just a few short years of youth, pleasure, and prosperity, and after that, just a blank, a void, with nothing apparently surviving – perhaps some ghostly wraith twittering in the darkness, but nothing more.

What could you do about it? It seemed that you could do nothing at all. Most people just tried to forget about it and enjoy life as much as possible while they could. 'Eat, drink, and be merry, for tomorrow we die,' expressed the substance of their philosophy. A few who were made of sterner stuff immersed themselves in action. They performed heroic deeds – went about slaying monsters, fighting battles, conquering kingdoms. They tried to make a name for themselves so that even though they might perish – probably sooner rather than later – their names would live on after them, so they hoped, for ever. But even these heroes, in their more reflective moments, saw that this was all a bit pointless.

Human life, it seemed, was not just a mystery, but a tragedy. This mood is reflected in the traditions and tales of ancient cultures, which were eventually written down to become the earliest examples of our literature. We find it in the Babylonian epic of Gilgamesh, from around 3000BCE, and in Homer's account of the fall of Troy, the *Iliad*, composed over 2,000 years later. It is there in the Anglo-Saxon epic poem *Beowulf*, dating from the eighth century, and it is perhaps even more powerfully and bitterly expressed in the Bible, in the Book of Ecclesiastes, the 'Book of the Preacher'. The vanity of human ambition in the face of death, the great leveller, is a favourite theme in ancient literature, and has inspired the same sort of thing in more recent times:

> *The boast of heraldry, the pomp of pow'r,*
> *And all that beauty, all that wealth e'er gave,*
> *Awaits alike th'inevitable hour:*
> *The paths of glory lead but to the grave.*[22]

But this was not the whole story. It was only half the story – the western half. Further east, people had started to take a different attitude, and had, in fact, arrived at some sort of solution to the mystery of death, which of course also meant some sort of solution to the mystery of life. What they perceived was that death was not the end. Human beings did not just vanish. After a time, they came back in a new body, in accordance with the nature of the deeds they had performed in their previous life. This perception made its first appearance in India at about the time of Homer (c.800BCE), and from India thereafter spread widely. The first clear reference to it is found in the *Brihadaranyaka Upanishad*, in which the idea is represented as a highly esoteric teaching, to be communicated only to the chosen few. But as the idea spread, it became known, in a more organized, systematized form, as the teaching of karma and rebirth.

When people in the West go flocking along to a lecture on karma and rebirth, or the *Tibetan Book of the Dead*, what they really want to know is: 'What is going to happen to me when I die? Is death the end, the absolute full stop, or not?' The fact is, if we could be assured that death was not the end, there would be no problem at all. If people knew with absolute certainty that they weren't going to just disappear when they died, they would be a lot less inclined to go and hear a lecture on karma and rebirth, or to snap up the latest commentary on the *Tibetan Book of the Dead*. For us, death is the problem. But in the East, especially the Hindu and Buddhist East, it is rather different. People are not so bothered about death there. For them, death is natural and inevitable – and so is rebirth. You die and you are reborn, you die again and you are reborn again – that's just the way it is. It's not a matter for speculation at all. In the East it is not death that is the problem. The problem is how to escape from the whole process of birth and death. How can you reach a state in which you will no longer be subject to birth and death? The problem is dying and being born time and time again, through endless ages. So the question is carried a stage further: what for the West is a solution of the problem is for the East a problem in itself, requiring a further solution. And this is where the Buddha's discovery of the universal principle of conditionality comes in.

When, in the course of the Enlightenment experience, the Buddha surveyed the whole vast range of conditioned existence, he saw that everything, from the lowest to the highest, was subject to the universal law of conditionality. And he also saw that this universal law operates – as we have already seen from the point of view of our evolutionary model – in two distinct modes: a cyclical mode and a spiral mode. In the cyclical mode, there is action and reaction between opposites. We experience pleasure and pain, vice and virtue, birth and death – and usually what happens is that we swing back and forth between them. Life is followed by death, which is in turn followed by new life. Pain is followed by pleasure which is again followed by pain. At all levels of life – physical, biological, psychological, sociological, historical – this same cyclical process can be found to be operating. Empires rise only to fall; growth must be succeeded by decay; health, wealth, fame, and status have old age, sickness, death, loss, and oblivion as their inevitable outcome.

In the spiral mode of conditionality, on the other hand, there is the possibility of real and permanent growth. Each factor in this process, rather than reversing the effect of the previous one, increases its effect. For example, instead of an oscillation between pleasure and pain, you go from pleasure to happiness, then from happiness to joy, from joy to rapture, from rapture to bliss, and so on indefinitely. And this spiral mode can be applied to life and death just as much as to anything else. The Buddha saw that as well as being subject to the endless round of birth and death, it was possible for human beings to enter the spiral path of spiritual development, which was 'the way to the door of the Deathless', the way beyond the opposites of life and death.

When applied to the process of life and death, the principle of conditionality gave rise to one of the most famous and important – and most frequently misunderstood – of Buddhist teachings: karma and rebirth. And this is the first thing to understand about karma, that this is all it is. It is just an application of the principle of conditionality. Nothing mysterious, nothing odd, nothing strange, nothing occult. Karma, in the most general terms, represents the law of conditionality at work on a certain plane of existence. This has to be emphasized, because one major source of confusion seems to be the idea that karma *is* the Buddhist teaching of cause and effect, and that it is universal – which is not the case. The universal principle is conditionality, and karma is only one of the ways in which conditionality operates. This point may be clarified by referring to a Buddhist teaching which actually dates from considerably later than the Buddha's own lifetime. It comes, in fact, from the analytical and systematizing philosophical tradition of the Abhidharma, and it is the teaching of what is called the five *niyamas*. These five *niyamas* are a very useful formulation because, as is the way with the Abhidharma, they draw together strands which are otherwise rather loose and disconnected as we find them in the original suttas.

The word *niyama* is a term common to Pali and Sanskrit meaning a natural law, a cosmic order. According to this teaching there are five of them, showing the law of cause and effect at work on five different levels. The first three are straightforward enough, as they can be related to Western sciences. Firstly, there's *utu-niyama*. *Utu* means non-living matter. Nowadays people are beginning to doubt whether there is any such thing as non-living matter, but let's call it that for the time being. In other words, this is the physical, inorganic order of existence. *Utu-niyama* is therefore the law of cause and effect as operative on the level of inorganic matter. It very roughly embraces the laws of physics and chemistry and associated disciplines.

The second *niyama* is *bīja-niyama*. *Bīja* means 'seed', so *bīja-niyama* deals with the world of living matter, the physical organic order whose laws constitute the science of biology.

Then there is *citta-niyama*. *Citta* is 'mind', so *citta-niyama* is conditionality as operative in the world of mind. The existence of this third *niyama*, therefore, implies that mental activity and development are not haphazard, but governed by laws. And it is important that we understand what this means. We are used to the idea of laws operating on the level of physics, chemistry, and biology, but we are not so used to the idea that similar laws might govern mental events. We are more inclined, in the West, to the view that mental events just happen, without any particular causation. To some extent and in some quarters, the influence of Freud has begun to shift this assumption, but the idea that mental phenomena arise in dependence on conditions is not one that has yet penetrated deeply into popular thinking. It is there in Buddhism, however, in this teaching of *citta-niyama*, the law of cause and effect as operative in the world of mind – and we may say that it is a concept which corresponds to the modern science of psychology.

Fourthly: *kamma-niyama*. *Kamma* (Pali) is of course more popularly known in its Sanskrit form, *karma*, and it means 'action', but in the sense of deliberately willed action. So it is traditionally, and paradoxically, said sometimes that karma is equivalent to *cetanā* (volitional consciousness), that is that action equals volition: 'for as soon as volition arises, one does the action, whether by body, speech, or mind.' *Kamma-niyama* therefore pertains to the world of ethical responsibility; it is the principle of conditionality operative on the moral plane.

It is perhaps difficult for those of us with a background of Western thought on morality to understand how this works. In ordinary social life, if you commit a crime, you are arrested and brought before the judge or magistrate, tried and convicted, sentenced, and sent to jail or fined. Committing the crime and being punished are quite separate events, and there is someone or something – society, the police, the judge, the law – who punishes you. Our tendency is to apply this legal model when it comes to morality as a whole. We think of sin and the *punishment* of sin, virtue and the *reward* of virtue. And traditionally we have tended to think in terms of a judge too: somebody who sees what you do, and punishes or rewards you accordingly – the judge being, of course, God. People imagine God as holding a sort of tremendous quarter sessions, with everybody hauled up in front of him, and the angels and demons standing around like police witnesses. It is still official Christian doctrine that when you die you face your judge, and this is a terrible thought for the orthodox Christian – that you are going to be put in the dock before the Transcendental Beak and then bundled off wherever he sends you. The dramatic possibilities inherent in the doctrine has made for some terrific literature, music, drama, and art – Michelangelo's tremendous painting of the Last Judgement in the Sistine Chapel is just one notable example. But it also makes for rather poor philosophy, and a mode of thinking from which we are still suffering a ghastly hangover.

The Buddhist point of view is totally different, and one that may seem distinctly odd to us, with our approach to ethics – almost whether we like it or not – underpinned by Christian theology. In Buddhism there is a law but no lawgiver, and no one who administers the law. I have heard Christian missionaries arguing with Buddhists and insisting that if you believe in a law, there must be a lawgiver – but of course this is quite specious. After all, there is a law of gravity, but there isn't a god of gravity pushing and pulling things. The law of gravity is just a generalized description of what happens when objects fall. In the same way we don't have a god of heredity, or a god of sexual selection. These things just happen; they work themselves.

It is much the same on the moral plane, according to Buddhism. The law administers itself, so to speak. Good karma naturally results in happiness, and bad karma naturally results in misery. There is no need for anybody else to come along, look at what you've done, and then fit the punishment or the reward to the deed. It happens of its own accord. 'Good' and 'bad' are built into the structure of the universe. This might sound dreadfully anthropomorphic – and we are putting it rather crudely here – but what it really means is that from the Buddhist point of view the universe is an ethical universe. Putting it more precisely, the universe functions according to conditionality, and this operates at the karmic level in a way which we could describe as ethical, in that it conserves ethical values. This is *kamma-niyama*.

The fifth and last *niyama* is *dhamma-niyama*. *Dhamma* (*dharma* in Sanskrit), which is a word with a number of different possible applications, here means simply spiritual or transcendental as opposed to mundane. So the principle of conditionality operates on this level too. Exactly how it does so, however, has not always been made very clear. It must be said that some of the more popular traditional explanations of this *niyama* are a bit childish and superficial. For example, many legends report that when the Buddha gained Enlightenment, and also when he died – and indeed on other momentous occasions – the earth shook and trembled in six different ways; and this, according to some commentators, was due to the operation of *dhamma-niyama*.

In fact we do not have to look very far in order to locate a more sensible and helpful interpretation. The obvious key, it seems to me at least, is in the distinction between the two types or modes of conditionality. The first four *niyamas*, including *kamma-niyama*, are all types of conditionality in the cyclical sense, in the sense of action and reaction between pairs of opposites. But *dhamma-niyama* corresponds to the spiral type of conditionality. As such it constitutes the sum total of the spiritual laws which govern progress through the stages of the Buddhist path.

Thus karma is not the law of conditionality in general, but only that law as operating on a certain level – the ethical level, the plane of moral responsibility. This means we cannot assume that what befalls us necessarily does so as a result of our past actions, because karma is only one of the five levels of conditionality. What happens to us may be a result of physical, biological, psychological, ethical, *or* spiritual factors. In all likelihood, it will involve a complex *combination* of factors, bringing several of the *niyamas* into play.

But how does karma actually work? If there is no judge handing out sentences, what does happen? The Abhidharma, that most precise school of Buddhist philosophy, gives us a very clear picture of karma, classifying it from seven different points of view. These are: ethical status; 'door' (what that means will be explained when we get to it); appropriateness of resultant experiences; time of taking effect; relative priority of taking effect; function; and the plane on which the karma matures. Let's look at these seven ways of classifying karma one by one.

Firstly, how is karma classified 'according to ethical status'? The main point to be grasped here is that the ethical status of a willed action is determined by the state of consciousness in which it is performed – this is absolutely axiomatic for Buddhism. This state of consciousness can be what Buddhists call 'skilful' or it can be what is called 'unskilful' – and this terminology is significant because it emphasizes that the practice of Buddhist ethics is a matter of intelligence as well as benevolence. Our unskilful mental states are those dominated by craving (neurotic desire), by aversion (hatred, resentment), and by ignorance. We are not punished for them – they simply make us miserable, inasmuch as unskilful states of mind involve a contraction of our being and consciousness which we experience as misery. Skilful mental states, by contrast, are characterized by contentment, love, understanding, and clarity of mind. And again, there are no prizes handed out to reward us for these. Skilful actions – whether of body, speech, or mind – result by themselves in a sense of expanded being and consciousness which we experience as happiness. In a sense, skilful action *is* happiness.

So Buddhist ethics are psychologically based. Action is skilful or unskilful not because it conforms with an external set of rules, but because it accords with a certain state of being. There are 'rules' – well, they are usually termed 'precepts'; they are rules only in the sense of being rough and ready guides to indicate the way you might normally behave if you were in a certain state of being. The 'rules' are not ends in themselves; they are not imposed by the religious 'group'; they are simply there to be of use towards a specific end, which is Enlightenment. The Buddha, moreover, distinguished between 'natural morality' (Pali *pakati-sīla*) and 'conventional morality' (*paṇṇatti-sīla*). Natural morality is universal, and based on the facts of human psychology, while conventional morality varies from place to place, and is based on custom and opinion. And it is only natural morality which comes under the operation of the law of karma.

Some schools of Buddhism are very much concerned to safeguard this psychological and spiritual basis of Buddhist ethics. In order to counter the danger of ethical formalism – the belief that you are good just because you are following the rule-book – Zen and the Tantric schools insist on drawing out a surprising, even shocking, implication of the Buddhist approach to morality. They go so far as to maintain that in principle the Enlightened man or woman is quite capable of committing apparently unethical actions. It is the state of consciousness that counts, they say, not the action itself, because it is the state of consciousness that determines the ethical value, and therefore the karmic effect, of the action – not the other way around. The way these Tantric and Zen schools look at it, such is our propensity to grasp at the easy answers provided by ethical formalism that we have to be positively scandalized into seeing that Buddhist ethics operate on a different basis from conventional morality. So they come up with some bizarre stories, of which one of the most extreme examples is the following from Tibet.

Once upon a time, so the tale begins, there was an ancient and holy hermit who lived all by himself in a mountain cave – and as this was Tibet we should probably imagine it as being just above the snow-line, thus bitterly cold. So he lived just like Milarepa, the famed poet and ascetic, except that he did not live just on nettles, which was Milarepa's staple diet. Though he was very strict and austere, he didn't live on nettles because just a few miles away there lived an old woman who used to supply him with meals every day, so that he could get on with his meditation without having to bother about food. Every day she used to approach the mouth of the cave, with great faith and devotion, and set the food down in front of the old hermit. He would eat it silently and give her a blessing. Then she would silently take away the empty dish and go back home, while he returned to his meditation.

This old lady had a daughter who was also devoted to the old ascetic, and sometimes she sent the girl to give the hermit his meal instead of going herself. One day the daughter went up as she often did and placed the food in front of the hermit. But this time, to her great surprise, instead of eating it quietly as usual, the hermit leapt up and tried to rape her. Considerably surprised, and even more considerably annoyed, she resisted his assault stoutly. As she was a hefty country wench, and the old hermit was feeble and weak, she had no trouble in beating him off and running home unscathed. 'Mother!' she cried, as soon as she had her breath back. 'What do you think? That old man we've been thinking all this while is so holy – what do you think he tried to do?' And she told her mother all about it. Her mother was certainly outraged, but for a quite unexpected reason. 'You foolish girl!' she scolded, 'You wicked girl! Have you no faith? A holy man like that does not try to rape someone for fun. There must have been some important meaning to it – don't you understand? Go back at once, apologize, and say "Here I am. Please do as you wish."'

So the girl went back and found the hermit sitting in front of his cave. She bowed in front of him and said, 'I am very sorry I was so foolish a little while ago. Here I am; I am at your service.' But the hermit said, 'You're too late!' She said, 'What do you mean? Too late for what?' And he said again, 'Too late! What a pity! Too late!' The girl was very puzzled, and asked again, 'Too late for what?' So the old hermit said, 'Well, since after all you were involved – or very nearly involved – I will tell you what was going on. You know just around the hill there's a big, wealthy monastery? Well, the abbot there was a very wicked man. He wasn't a good monk at all. He didn't care about the Dharma, he never studied anything, and he was very greedy for money and food and possessions.

'Now the fact is, the abbot died just a few hours ago, and as I was meditating, I saw his spirit hovering in the air. It was in a terrible condition, so sad and miserable, and I could see that it was gravitating towards a lower birth, a really unpleasant future life. There were no other people around, but at that moment you turned up. Out of compassion I wanted to give that unhappy spirit one more chance. I thought, "If I move fast perhaps I can help him at least to be reborn as a human being." But unfortunately you ran away – and do you know what happened? In that field over there, just after you left, two donkeys copulated – and so, yes, you are too late! The abbot will be reborn as a donkey.'

The Tibetans tell this story whenever they get the chance. It's one of their favourites – and it does illustrate the point. It is, indeed, the sheer unlikelihood of a compassionate act of rape that makes the point. Whatever the ethical rule, however straightforward it may seem, though it may cover many, many instances, it can never be regarded as absolute. The state of consciousness in which an action is performed is what determines its ethical value.

Of course, this teaching – though it is crucial – can easily be misunderstood. It is only too easy to make it mean 'If it feels good, do it,' – but this is a complete distortion of the Buddhist ethic. After all, quite a lot of people feel good even when they are doing something which is unskilful in every sense. It's not a question of following your instincts or feelings willy-nilly, but of trying to achieve the most positive mental state possible and acting from that. The ethical 'rules' or precepts are always there to provide a guide to the kind of action that will support positive mental states, even when your mental states are less than positive. But the ideal, the aim of Buddhist ethics, is to succeed in acting from a positive, skilful mental state – one of contentment, love, compassion, peace, tranquillity, joy, wisdom, awareness, and clarity of understanding. So much for the classification of karma according to ethical status.

Next, the classification of karma according to 'door'. This picturesque expression refers to the door through which, as it were, the karma is performed. Traditionally, Buddhism divides the human being into three aspects: body, speech, and mind – these are the doors. For it is not only physical actions and actions in the form of speech that have karmic consequences. Mental actions, that is, thoughts and feelings, do too. In fact, any action, of whatever kind, will only have a karmic effect if it is intentional. If you didn't mean to do something, or if what you say is misinterpreted, that action does not produce effects under the law of karma. Here Buddhism differs from Jainism. Jainism holds that if, for example, you take life by accident – even if you have taken all possible precautions against doing so – that action still has karmic consequences which will cause you to suffer in the future. In other words, the Jain system of ethics is based on rules – very complicated rules – whereas the Buddhist system is based on psychology.

Thirdly, karma can be classified 'according to the appropriateness of resultant experiences'. Putting it crudely – and indeed unbuddhistically

– this is saying that karma works by making the punishment fit the crime. For example, if you adopt an attitude of reverence for life, if you guard and protect living beings, you will be reborn in a state of happiness in which you will enjoy long life. If, on the contrary, you deliberately take life, you will be reborn in a state of suffering, and your life will be short. In the same way, if you practise generosity, you will be reborn in comfortable circumstances, but if you are mean, you will be reborn poor and destitute. If you show respect and honour for others, you will be reborn in a high social position, but if you look down on others and treat them with contempt, you will be reborn at the bottom of the social scale.

Sometimes this principle is applied in a way that may seem to us in the West a bit ludicrous. For instance, one of the texts says that if you slander others, if you gossip unkindly about other people, you will be reborn suffering from halitosis. There's also the story of the Arhant who was born a dwarf. Apparently the Buddha had a disciple who was a dwarf. He was Enlightened, his Dharma knowledge was immense, he was a wonderful preacher – but he was a dwarf, and a hunchback too. The story goes that one day the Buddha's disciples began to discuss the case of this dwarf. He must have done many good things in previous lives to have been reborn as a disciple of the Buddha, but what could he possibly have done to be born a dwarf? To satisfy their curiosity, the Buddha is supposed to have told the following story.

Thousands and thousands of years ago, in a certain remote world period, there was a Buddha, in fact a *pratyekabuddha* – that is, a 'private' Buddha, one who gains Enlightenment but does not teach. When this Buddha died, the whole community decided to erect a magnificent monument to commemorate his life. As they discussed the project, some people said the monument should be twenty feet high, while others thought it should be at least forty feet high. And as this discussion was going on, the person who was to be reborn as a dwarf came along and said, 'What on earth does it matter? Surely a small monument will do.' It was as a result of that very bad karma that he was reborn as a dwarf.

I remember this story being told very solemnly in a Burmese Buddhist magazine. At the time some Buddhists – I was one of them – were suggesting that instead of spending all their spare cash gilding monuments, the Burmese might usefully devote some of it to printing books on Buddhism. They trotted out this apocryphal story to show the terrible karmic consequences we were apparently creating for ourselves by suggesting such a thing, and it just shows the rather silly way in which this principle has sometimes been applied. Despite such slightly tendentious applications, however, the principle holds good. The principle is, in fact, quite clear. We could put it another way: whatever we do to other people, we are in the long run also doing to ourselves. This is not just Buddhist theology; it's good sound psychology. We could even put it the other way round and say that whatever we do to ourselves, we are in the long run doing to other people.

The fourth way of classifying karma is 'according to time of taking effect'. In this sense, there are three kinds of karma: those which take effect in the present life – that is, the results accrue during the life in which the action was committed; those which take effect in a subsequent life; and those which do not take effect at all. This third category may come as a surprise. In some popular expositions, the idea is put forward that karma is an iron law from which nothing escapes. It is suggested that even if you did a very small action – good or bad – millions of years ago in some remote existence, it will catch up with you in the end. And this is clearly an idea that appeals strongly to some people – that you never escape, that you will ultimately have to pay for everything you have done.

It is not, however, the Buddhist teaching. According to Buddhism, some karmas, whether skilful or unskilful, are just cancelled out in the course of time. They may be counterbalanced by opposite karmas, or simply lose their force. Lacking an opportunity for expression, they may just fade away. So there is no 'iron law' of karma; some karmas do not produce any effect at all.

The fifth way of ordering karma – 'according to relative priority of taking effect' – brings us to the question of rebirth. Rebirth is the result of karma, but karma is of many different kinds. When you have died and are about to be reborn, there are all sorts of karmas in the background crowding in, so to speak, waiting to produce their effect. So the question addressed here is this: in what order of priority do they influence the nature of your rebirth?

According to this mode of classification, karmas basically line up in four groups of relative priority. Firstly, under the heading of 'weighty' karma are gathered those karmas which embody conscious volitions, whether skilful or unskilful, which are so strong that they modify and affect your whole character. The example usually given of an unskilful weighty karma is that of the deliberate taking of life – murder – especially if the victim is spiritually advanced. An important skilful weighty karma, on the other hand, is meditation. But you have to be clear what this means here, because the word seems to be more often used, even among Buddhists, in the sense of *trying* to meditate, rather than in the sense of actually experiencing higher states of consciousness. As a skilful weighty karma, meditation is not just a dreamy, passive sort of wool-gathering. It is an action which modifies your whole being, your whole character, your whole consciousness, both here and now, and in the future. When you have been meditating you shouldn't end up in a sweet, gentle, slightly abstracted state of mind. If you do, you may have been having a pleasant little reverie, but it will not have been meditation. Meditation is something much more dynamic, more challenging, even more shattering; afterwards, you should feel full of power and energy and life. So weighty karma, whether skilful or unskilful, exerts a tremendous influence.

Second in the scale of influence over one's rebirth is 'death-proximate' karma. This means a sort of mental image which appears at the time of death, usually one which connects in some way with your activities and interests in life. The example commonly given in this regard is that of the butcher, who, we are told, is very likely to see visions of slaughter at the time of his or her death. So he or she may well see an animal being butchered, or hear its cries, and see blood and meat cleavers: obviously, his or her mental state will not then be a very happy one. A painter, by contrast, might see beautiful forms – colours and shapes – while a musician might hear music. Whatever you experience, however, does not necessarily have to be connected with your previous life. The image you see at this time may alternatively be connected with the place of your future rebirth. If you see a beautiful lotus flower, white or pink or golden, this is said to indicate rebirth on a higher plane of consciousness, a 'heaven realm'. If, on the other hand, you see flames, this of course indicates rebirth in another place.

The third category of karma which has an effect at this time is 'habitual' karma, that is, any action which one has repeated a number of times during one's life. A very great part of one's life is probably made up of habitual karmas, things we do over and over again, often without realizing the effect they are having on us. The action itself may not amount to very much – it may not take up much time – but if we do it every day, perhaps several times a day, it has its effect, like drops of water wearing away a stone. All the time we are creating karma, either forging a sort of chain which binds us, or planting seeds of future growth. And it need not necessarily be repeated physical action. Even an action which we do only once, but on which we continually reflect, mentally re-enacting it again and again – this also counts as habitual karma. There is no need to offer examples of this, I am sure.

The fourth and last class of karma, distinguished 'according to relative priority of taking effect', is called 'residual' karma, which constitutes any willed action not included under the other three headings. The Abhidharma is nothing if not tidy.

So when we are between death and rebirth, between one life and another, hovering on the brink, these karmas come into effect and determine the nature of our rebirth in this order. According to the Abhidharma, the weighty karmas take effect first. If you have to your debit or credit a weighty karma, it is this that will decide initially the kind of rebirth you will have. One can now begin to appreciate the importance of meditation from the karmic point of view. If you have meditated much during your life, if you have dwelt in a higher state of consciousness consistently, or even from time to time, or even once – if you have really penetrated to some higher level of being during your lifetime, even for just a few minutes – it is that factor which will initially determine the nature of your future rebirth. Other factors will take effect afterwards.

If, however, you have drawn no weighty karma, either skilful or unskilful, in your previous life, your rebirth is determined by the death-proximate karma. In the absence of death-proximate karma, it is determined by habitual karma, and in the absence even of habitual karma – this would be very unusual – it is determined by residual karma. At least, some Abhidharma authorities give this order of priority, while others say that habitual karma takes precedence over death-proximate karma – but despite this difference of opinion, the general picture is clear.

Karmas can overlap these categories, of course: a particular karma could function in all these ways. For instance, if you have meditated during your lifetime, that's a weighty karma. If at the time of your death you think of that meditation experience, it becomes a death-proximate karma. And if during your lifetime you have meditated many, many times, it will also be a habitual karma. If meditation is your weighty karma, your death-proximate karma, and also your habitual karma, then obviously meditation is going to be very much the determining factor when it comes to your next rebirth. You are likely, according to Buddhism, to be reborn in a higher state of consciousness, even in a higher world, than before: you will be virtually a born yogi, living in a world fit for yogis to live in.

The sixth classification of karma, after 'according to relative priority of taking effect', is 'according to function'. This refers to a fourfold disposition of karmas: 'reproductive', 'supportive', 'counteractive', and 'destructive'. Reproductive karmas are those which are directly responsible for the production of a new life after death. So this category refers to the way we create tendencies which will result in our being reborn, the way we indulge our craving, aversion, and ignorance. Supportive karma refers to the way we set up and reinforce those tendencies. Counteractive karma refers to the process by which the effects of our actions can be offset, countered, or cancelled by other actions. Thus weighty positive karma like meditative concentration would be counteractive karma inasmuch as it cancelled out weighty negative karma like gross breaches of the ethical precepts. Finally, destructive karma is any experience of Insight into Reality sustained deeply enough to destroy negative karma at the root.

There is a traditional simile which illustrates this classification. Reproductive karma is compared to a seed planted in a field – the new life is, as it were, 'planted' in the mother's womb. Supportive karma is like the rain and manure that nourish the seed and help it to grow into a plant. Counteractive karma is like a hailstorm that falls upon the growing crops and damages them. And destructive karma is like fire that burns up the whole field so that the crop perishes. So from the point of view of function, karmas are of these four kinds.

The seventh and last classification of karma is 'according to the plane on which the karma matures'. This is very important, and again it is closely connected with the whole question of rebirth. In the Buddhist world picture, the universe is conceived in terms of space-time and also in terms of what we might call depth, or the spiritual dimension. Space-time represents the objective, material aspect of conditioned existence, whereas the spiritual dimension represents its mental, subjective aspect. The first of these aspects we usually refer to as the world or sphere or plane in which we exist, while the second we refer to as our state of mind or experience of that existence. In the microcosm of the individual human being these two poles or dimensions are represented by body and mind, body being the human entity in terms of space and time, and mind being the same human entity in terms of depth or spiritual dimension.

All this is illustrated by the *Tibetan Book of the Dead*, which, among other things, tries to answer the question 'What happens when we die?' It describes how the senses gradually fail. You no longer hear, or see, or smell, or taste, or feel. Eventually consciousness detaches itself from the body. The body loses its heat. Then even the subtle psychic link which exists between the body and its non-material aspects snaps. At that point you are really and truly dead. And then – according to the Buddhist teaching exemplified in great detail by the *Tibetan Book of the Dead* – in that first instant after you are completely dead, you find yourself face to face with Reality itself. It is as though throughout your life the body, the senses, the lower mind, sheltered you from Reality all the time, shutting it out, or at least filtering it, so that you only experienced a very little of it at a time. But after death, when the body is no longer there, when the lower mind is no longer there, or is at least suspended, Reality dawns, and flashes upon you for one dreadful instant. I say 'dreadful' because most people cannot bear it – they shrink back in terror. 'Human kind', as T.S. Eliot puts it, 'cannot bear very much reality.'[23]

When the human consciousness finds itself face to face with Reality, this can be a terrifying experience from which the mind flees, retreating to lower and ever lower levels until at last it finds itself on a level where it feels at home. On that level it grasps a body, and in that body it is then, as we say, 'reborn'. Of course, we should not be misled by words. We speak of the consciousness coming and going – we even speak of it passing from one body to another – but there is no real coming and going of consciousness. It does not occupy space in a literal sense; it cannot 'enter' a body. Mind and body are like the two ends of a stick: you grasp one and the other automatically follows.

So these are the seven classifications of karma, and together with the five *niyamas* they give a comprehensive picture of the nature of karma. Karma is one's own deliberately willed action and the results which follow from that, as well as the law by virtue of which the one follows upon the other. It is not fate; it is not destiny. Neither is it the law of cause and effect in general. As the teaching of the five *niyamas* makes clear, karma is just one kind of conditionality – albeit a very important one – along with four others. It is therefore wrong to say that whatever happens is the result of karma. Some people imagine that if, when something happens to them, they say, 'Ah well, that must be my karma,' they are being very pious, very Buddhist – but this is not in fact the Buddhist teaching. Buddhism teaches that whatever happens happens as a result of conditions, but that not all those conditions are karma. Karma is only one among the five kinds of conditionality at work in the universe. Events may be the result of karma, or they may not. How we find out is another question altogether.

A difficulty that crops up sometimes is the relationship between rebirth and the *anātman* teaching, the teaching that there is no self, or no soul. One might think, 'If there is no soul which passes from one life, one body, to another, how does rebirth take place?' It might seem that you've got to sacrifice either the *anātman* doctrine or the teaching of rebirth – you can't have both. But this is an artificial difficulty. *Anātman* does not, as we have said in our opening chapter, actually mean no soul in the sense of no psychic life at all. It means no *unchanging* soul, no *unchanging* self. When it comes to rebirth, there is a substratum of mental activity that 'flows' from life to life – now linked with this body, now with that. It is the linking of a fresh body with this 'stream' of mental activity that constitutes what we call rebirth. So there is no contradiction; you can have *anātman* and rebirth side by side.

By this stage in a discussion of karma one can sometimes find oneself thinking, 'It's all very well. It hangs together beautifully. It all sounds very plausible. But is it true? How can we know? What is the proof?' The average Western mind wants 'hard' evidence, and this is slowly but assiduously being gathered. Teams of researchers are systematically investigating the cases of people who claim to be able to remember their previous lives. Records are gathered and published of ordinary people – not saints or sages or meditators – who claim, for no apparent reason, to remember a previous life. They usually go into all the details, too – their name, where they lived, what they did, what illness they died of, and so on. And it seems that these details are found to tally with what is still known about the lives – ordinary humdrum lives for the most part – that they claim to recall. The scientists tend to be particularly interested in the many cases of curious recollections of this kind on the part of children. The possibility of coincidence or fraud or imagination has been ruled out completely in many cases, and researchers seem inclined to admit that a hypothesis of rebirth, or reincarnation, would provide the simplest explanation for the facts. As more and more evidence of this sort comes to light, I have no doubt that it will eventually convince all open-minded people of the truth of the teaching of karma and rebirth.

Some people point to further evidence for karma and rebirth in the existence of child prodigies. When you get a child like the young Mozart who could play, sing, and compose at a very tender age, it is hard to believe that this degree of knowledge and proficiency could possibly have been acquired entirely in the present life; it must, so it is argued, have been carried over from a previous life. But this brings up the whole question of heredity: there is no general agreement as to what can and cannot be inherited in the genes. The issue is complicated besides by all sorts of other factors, both personal and cultural, so that particular line of argument is hardly as convincing as the evidence of recollection.

The idea of karma and rebirth certainly resolves many more questions and problems than it creates, but this is not to say that there are no loose ends in the teaching. In my opinion, the traditional doctrine needs a thorough reformulation, taking account of various matters that have not so far, apparently, been considered in the East. For instance, there is the whole question of the relation between karma and rebirth and time, and between karma and rebirth and the individual consciousness. Karma and rebirth operate within time – so what is time? Karma and rebirth pertain to the individual consciousness – so what is that? There is also the knotty question of population explosion. Where have all the people come from? Has there been a sort of fission of souls, or have they come from other realms, or other worlds? Some Eastern Buddhists would say loftily, 'Of course they have come from other realms and worlds. Everybody knows that.' But is this the only possible solution? These and similar questions will have to be given full consideration in a new formulation of the traditional Buddhist teaching of karma and rebirth; and this reformulation will perhaps be one of the works of Western Buddhism.

In the end, we have to admit that there will be for some time, perhaps, a certain amount of resistance from many quarters in the West to the idea of karma and rebirth. As we have seen, it cuts across a lot of our Western assumptions about some of our deepest concerns. So an important question for a lot of people is this: do you have to believe in karma and rebirth to be a Buddhist? The simple answer is 'Yes.' But an answer which might be more illuminating is 'No – but on one condition. You need not believe in karma and rebirth provided that you are willing to go all out for full Enlightenment in this life.' This is certainly true, and might satisfy some people. But it also shows at once how difficult it might be to practise Buddhism seriously without installing karma and rebirth as part of one's mental furniture, so to speak.

The teaching of karma and rebirth does provide an answer – perhaps *the* answer – to certain questions. It helps to solve the mystery of death, which is also the mystery of life – and very few people can follow the path to Enlightenment without bothering, at least sometimes, about such questions. A few may be happy to get on with their meditation and not worry about philosophy, but most people require some answers. They really want to know, and it is only within the framework of this sort of knowledge that they can practise at all. They need to have some general philosophical framework, however rudimentary or sketchy, within which to follow the path. The teaching of karma and rebirth does give, at least in part, such a framework.

If we do not accept karma and rebirth as a solution, we are going to have to find another one, and that, I think, will not be easy. I personally believe that the teaching of karma and rebirth is the most satisfactory answer to many of the questions raised by the fact of death and the nature of human life and existence. It is not only true; it gives meaning and purpose to life. It makes it clear that human beings are pilgrims through a succession of lives, and that by changing our consciousness – something which is, according to Buddhism, very much within our power – we can determine our own destiny, not only in this life, but in future lives as well. This means that no real effort is ever wasted. The good is conserved from life to life. There is no question of reward, and there is no question of punishment. By performing a consciously willed action we modify our own consciousness, both here and now, and for the future – and that is surely reward or punishment enough. I would say personally that the teaching of karma and rebirth is an integral part of Buddhism, and that for most people it would be difficult to be a Buddhist without accepting it, at least in principle.

Traditionally, the truth of the teaching of karma and rebirth is said to become clear in the light of higher states of consciousness, and especially in that highest of all states of consciousness – so high that it is not really to be called a state of consciousness as such – the Enlightenment of a Buddha. In the East it is held that there are some truths – call them 'spiritual truths' if you like – that cannot be perceived by the ordinary rational mind.

This, of course, is a point of view that we in the West usually find completely unacceptable. We tend to take it for granted that anything that can be understood or seen can be understood or seen by our ordinary conscious 'everyday' mind. This mind, we assume, is capable of understanding anything that can be understood at all. But Eastern tradition, especially Indian tradition, says that there are some truths – some laws or principles, if you like – which cannot be understood by the ordinary human mind. If you want to understand them you have to raise your level of consciousness, in the same way that if you want to see a long way you have to climb a mountain. Buddhists take the view that if you climb the mountainside of your own consciousness you will see, spread out before you, as it were, spiritual truths which in your ordinary state of consciousness you could not have perceived.

According to Indian tradition, the teaching of karma and rebirth is one of these truths. Our ordinary, rational consciousness cannot apprehend it. We may be able to understand it when it is explained to us, but we cannot really see the truth of it directly. Karma and rebirth in all their details, all their workings, all their ramifications, are perceived only by a Buddha. This means that the hard facts, as it were, are not really available to us.

However, in the course of the thousands of years of the development of Buddhism, all the Buddhist sages and yogis have testified to the truth of karma and rebirth. There has never been a school of Buddhism or a prominent Buddhist teacher who has questioned it – which is interesting. If the teaching of karma and rebirth had been just a doctrine, a philosophical idea, a speculation, surely someone in the Buddhist world at some time would have denied it, or at least doubted it? Buddhists have complete freedom of thought – there is no ecclesiastical power to coerce them into orthodoxy – so Buddhist history is full of the questioning of doctrine. Why, then, has the teaching of karma and rebirth never, apparently, been questioned? I suggest that this is because karma and rebirth is not a matter of speculation and philosophy, but one of experience and perception. As the great yogis and meditators increased in spiritual understanding and insight, they would have seen more and more clearly the truth of this teaching. They may not have perceived it as fully as the Buddha did, but they saw enough of it to be convinced of its truth. So in the East the evidence of the superconscious perception of the Buddha and other Enlightened teachers is considered conclusive proof of the truth of karma and rebirth. For practising Buddhists, at least, this should provide sufficient basis for their faith until they can perceive the truth of karma and rebirth directly for themselves.

Karma and rebirth are complex subjects, but some understanding of the teaching is essential to an understanding of who the Buddha is. The Buddha's primary Insight into the nature of Reality, the realization of which made him who he was, arose out of his direct perception of the workings of karma and rebirth. On the night of his Enlightenment, as he was seated beneath the bodhi tree, the Buddha saw, in a flash of illumination, the whole series of his previous existences – tens of thousands of previous lives. Not only that: he could see, stretching back into the past, the previous lives of other living beings – and on that night, and whenever he wished subsequently, he could see their future existences too. The Buddha taught the doctrine of karma and rebirth not as a philosophical teaching, something he had worked out logically, but as something he had experienced, something he had seen. This faculty, this ability to see previous lives, one's own and other people's, is technically known as *pūrvanivāsā-smṛti* – literally 'recollection of previous abodes'. It is reckoned as one of the five or six *abhijñās*, the 'superknowledges', and we are told that it can be cultivated on the basis of the practice of meditation by anybody who cares to make the effort.

8

The 'Death' of the Buddha

The 'death' of the Buddha wasn't an ordinary death, because the Buddha was not an ordinary person. Even during his lifetime, his very closest disciples were sometimes perplexed by the question of the Buddha's nature. Who was the Buddha? What was the Buddha? And what would happen to the Buddha when he died? We don't know why, but apparently in the days of the Buddha quite a lot of the disciples, and quite a lot of members of the public, were very interested in this last question. So many people, indeed, seem to have been fascinated by it that there came to be a standard way of putting it. People used to come to the Buddha and say, 'Lord, after death, does the Tathāgata (that is to say the Buddha) exist, or does he not exist, or both, or neither?' And the Buddha would always give the same reply. He would always say, 'It is inappropriate to say of a Buddha that after death he exists. It is inappropriate to say of a Buddha that after death he does not exist. It is inappropriate to say of a Buddha that after death he both exists (in one sense) and does not exist (in another). And it is inappropriate to say of a Buddha that after death he neither exists nor does not exist. All ways of telling, all ways of describing, are totally inapplicable to the Buddha.'[24]

From this it becomes clear that the Buddha's death is not death in the ordinary sense at all. This is why in the Buddhist tradition it is usually termed the *parinirvāṇa*. We don't say the Buddha died; we say he attained *parinirvāṇa*. Nirvāṇa, of course, means Enlightenment, and *pari* means 'supreme', so *parinirvāṇa* means 'supreme Enlightenment'. What then is the difference between nirvāṇa and *parinirvāṇa*? Well, none at all, really. When a Buddha attains nirvāṇa, this is traditionally called the 'nirvāṇa with remainder', because the Buddha still has a physical body. *Parinirvaṇa*, on the other hand, is known as the 'nirvāṇa without remainder' because the physical body is then no longer attached. This is the only difference – and this difference only affects other people, notably his unenlightened disciples. The nirvāṇa is just the same. From the Buddha's point of view, there is no difference at all between the two states. Before death or after death, the experience, whatever it is – and we cannot know or describe it – is exactly the same.

His attainment of *parinirvāṇa* may not have been an event of much consequence to the Buddha personally, but it is important to those of us who are unenlightened. His last days are recorded in the Pali canon in greater detail than any other part of his life after his Enlightenment. His followers evidently thought that the way he died taught them a great deal about him, about his teaching, and about the nature of Buddhahood.

He felt the sharp pains of his final sickness come upon him in a village near the great city of Vaiśālī. It may have been the sudden change in the weather with the beginning of the rainy season that brought them on. But by an effort of will he recovered sufficiently to undertake a gruelling 'farewell tour'. 'My journey is drawing to its close,' he said to Ānanda. 'Just as a worn-out carriage can only be kept going by being held together with straps, so this body can only be kept going by being strapped up. But my mental and spiritual vigour is undiminished.'[25] His body, like all conditioned things, was subject to decay, but his mind was beyond birth and death.

Taking leave of his disciples in Vaiśālī – a city very close to his heart – he set off on a final round of visits to other places where he would be able to offer some last words of encouragement. Despite the constant physical pain he endured, and despite his knowledge of his impending death, he was as outward-going and concerned with the needs of others as he had ever been. The scriptures also note that he was as aware of his surroundings as he had ever been, expressing an appreciation of the beauty of certain places they passed through, certain groves where they rested. He delivered discourses in towns and villages, continued to accept new disciples, and issued his final instructions to the Sangha. Reaching a village called Pāvā, he took what was to be his last meal, provided for him by the local smith, called Cunda. It gave him severe dysentery. With the last of his physical strength he made the journey to a place called Kuśinagara, in north-eastern India. Resting by a river on the way, he told Ānanda to comfort and reassure Cunda the smith that he should not be troubled in his mind at having inadvertently given the Buddha food poisoning. So far from being blameworthy, to provide a Buddha with his last meal before his *parinirvāṇa* was in fact highly meritorious.

Just as he was born in the open air under a tree and gained Enlightenment in the open air under a tree, so the Buddha attained *parinirvāṇa* in the open air under a tree. There are shrines, places of pilgrimage, at the site of each of these events, and the shrine to the *parinirvāṇa* is at Kuśinagara. The scriptures make it clear that Kuśinagara was honoured in this way by no kind of accident. It was his conscious choice to die in this 'miserable little town of wattle and daub in the back of beyond', as Ānanda rather fretfully called it. The Buddha was no more a victim of circumstance in his death as in any other aspect of his life.

Just outside Kuśinagara was a grove of sāl trees. Here the local people had built a stone couch for the elder of the village assembly to sit on. On this couch the Buddha lay down. He then sorted out the funeral arrangements: Ānanda and the other monks were not to concern themselves with it at all, but just get on with their spiritual practice. The lay followers, however, were to be enjoined to deal with his remains as they would those of a great king.

All this proved too much for Ānanda to bear, and he went away and wept. The Buddha called him back and said, 'Enough, Ānanda. Do not grieve so. It is in the very nature of all things most near and dear to us that at some time or other we must be parted from them. For a long time, Ānanda, you have shown unstinting and wholehearted loving-kindness to me in your actions, your speech, and your thoughts. Maintain your practice and you will surely attain liberation from the defilements.' The Buddha then extolled Ānanda's virtues before the whole company of monks.

After this the Buddha dealt with one or two points concerning monastic discipline. For example, he instructed that his old charioteer, Channa, who had joined the order but had proved wilfully errant in his practice, should be 'sent to Coventry' until he came to his senses –

which he did eventually. In this way the Buddha was able to focus his mind with clarity and compassion on the welfare of specific individuals right up to the end. Indeed, his last address to the monks amounted to an invitation to any individuals among them with doubts or uncertainties about his teaching to bring them up there and then, while he was still there to resolve them. When the company remained silent, he uttered his last exhortation: 'Decay is inherent in all conditioned things. With diligence, strive on.'[26] Then he entered into meditation and passed away.

The force of this final scene, more than any other in the Buddha's life, is most tellingly captured, not so much in the words of the Pali canon, but in the paintings by the great Chinese and Japanese artists of the medieval period. Against a beautiful forest backdrop, the trunks of the sāl trees are seen rising like columns, straight and tall, to a crown of broad green leaves and large white flowers. The Buddha is resting on his right side, with the sāl trees showering white blossoms down upon him. He is surrounded by disciples, his closest followers sitting near his head in their yellow robes, and all sorts of other people – Brahmins, princes, ministers, ascetics, fire worshippers, merchants, peasants, traders – crowding round where they can. Not only people, all sorts of animals as well – elephants, goats, deer, horses, dogs, even mice and birds – have gathered to look their last on the Buddha. Up in the clouds the gods and goddesses complete this cosmic deathbed scene. What comes across, therefore, from the best paintings of that scene is that this is no ordinary conclusion to someone's life, but an event of universal significance which the whole of creation has come to witness.

The general mood is, as you would expect, tearful. Even the animals are weeping, and you particularly notice the elephant's big, fat tears rolling down his cheek. In fact, the only ones who aren't weeping are a few of the disciples, those sitting closest to the Buddha, and the cat. The cat remains unmoved out of fabled feline nonchalance, but the closest disciples stay perfectly calm because they are able to see beyond the physical body, and know that really the change from nirvāṇa to *parinirvāṇa* is no change at all.

This is the scene, memorialized by many great artists, which Buddhists bring to mind each year on Parinirvāṇa Day, held on 15 February. It is, of course, a day of grateful celebration for the example and teaching of the Buddha's life. However, the mood is different from that of other festivals, because the real point of commemorating this event is to focus our minds on the fact of death – and not just the Buddha's 'death', but our own. So the mood is sober – not sombre but reflective, meditative. We reflect, indeed, that the fact of death is present not on one day of the year only, but every day of our lives, and that the recollection of this fact should be an intrinsic aspect of our daily spiritual practice. The Buddha's *parinirvāṇa* reminds us to renew our whole meditation practice in the light of the ever-present reality of death. But in particular it can spur us to take up meditation practices which are specifically concerned with death.

There is, of course, such a thing as an unhealthy, morbid fascination with death, and we have to be clear that the recollection of death as a meditation practice bears no relation to anything like an unwholesome or gloomy mental habit. It should, in fact, be undertaken on the basis of a highly positive and clear mind. As the development of mindfulness and positivity are the specific province of other practices, meditation on death cannot properly be presented except in the context of a systematic approach to meditation. In the course of this chapter, therefore, we shall be seeing where the recollection of death fits in with other methods of meditation.

Initially, we will look at the general nature of meditative experience, its function and purpose – that is, the sort of ground meditation covers – before going on to examine the various specific practices by which we enter upon that experience. In short, we will answer the question 'What do we mean by meditation?' The word is in common usage nowadays, but most people would be hard pressed to say what it is really all about.

Very broadly speaking, the word meditation can be used in three main senses, corresponding to three successively higher levels of experience. First of all, there is meditation in the sense of the integration – the bringing together – of all our psychic energies. This is the first step. Human beings, like other living things, are essentially embodiments of energy. We may not always look like it, but this is what we essentially are. The reason we don't always look like embodiments of energy is that we are split, our energy is split, into many different streams. Some flow in one direction, some in another, some meander happily, others rush and pour and tumble. A lot of the time these different streams of energy, instead of flowing together harmoniously, move in opposite directions. The result is either a whirlpool or stagnation: a lot of energy rushing around going nowhere, or a total energy shut-down. Because we are struggling against ourselves, divided within ourselves, our energies cancel each other out. This is a not uncommon state for people to find themselves in, their energies so scattered and distracted that they cannot do very much or achieve very much.

The first function of meditation, then, is to bring all these energies together and get them flowing in the same channel, get them flowing more and more smoothly and sharply, cutting deeper and deeper into this single channel so that it carries those energies more and more surely and steadily towards their goal. Gradually through meditating we integrate all our psychophysical energies, so that there is no longer any conflict or discord, and we experience peace and harmony and a sense of everything coming together.

The next level of experience to which we refer when we speak of meditation is the experience of superconscious states, termed within the Indian tradition *dhyānas*. These are states of progressive superconscious simplification. What this means is that – according to tradition, supported by the experience of anyone who puts in the work – you experience in the first dhyāna a number of mental factors, and this number is progressively reduced as you move into the three higher dhyānas.

In the first dhyāna, you experience not only integration – carried over from meditation in the previous sense – but also bliss and joy, as well as subtle mental activity of various kinds. But as you ascend to the second dhyāna, the mental activity gradually fades away. You don't think *of* anything, you don't think *about* anything. All mental functioning in this sense entirely ceases. But although the mind is stilled in this way, at the same time you are perfectly aware, perfectly conscious – more aware and more conscious than ever. The mind becomes like a vast lake in which every ripple has died away. Instead of being tossed into waves, it's perfectly calm, level, shining, and serene. At the same time it is as if the lake is being fed by an underground spring, so that you may experience degrees of intense but subtle psychophysical pleasure and joy welling up as certain energies are released. This is the experience of the second dhyāna.

Just as the mental activity faded away to give rise to the second dhyāna, so, on the higher level of the third dhyāna, even the experience of joy, which is comparatively coarse, fades away, and what you have left is simply intense bliss and peace. Then eventually there is not even a feeling of bliss. At this fourth level all the elements of your being, all your energies, are unified in a sort of vast ocean of integration, of mental harmony, with an overwhelming knowledge of absolute peace which far surpasses any experience of happiness or even bliss.

In this way the dhyānas develop from lower to higher and ever higher levels of experience, and one should be prepared for all sorts of things to happen on the way. What I've described represents a standard pattern, but there are all sorts of additional dimensions, all sorts of byways of experience which people may find themselves entering, according to their different temperaments and backgrounds. Some people have visions of archetypal images: visionary landscapes float before them; jewel-like forms, mandalas, even gods, goddesses, Buddhas, and Bodhisattvas emerge, as it were, from the depths of their own minds. Then again, other people, as they progress through the dhyānas, can discover various supernormal faculties developing – telepathy, for example. They may find they are aware of what is going on in other people's minds, or at least uncannily sensitive to how other people are feeling. They may hear or see things going on in other places. Some people even have the odd flash of what seems to be a recollection of a previous life.

Whatever unusual side-effects meditation may throw up, the Buddhist tradition is quite clear about how to deal with them. Basically, you don't. You pay no particular attention to them. In general, you treat them as a very subtle form of distraction from the job in hand, which is to try to extend and deepen your experience of meditation by moving from the lower to the higher dhyānas.

The third and highest level of meditative experience is that of insight into the true nature of existence. As higher levels of consciousness become more familiar, your experience becomes not only more integrated, blissful, and peaceful, but also more and more objective. You become less and less influenced by your own subjectivity, less and less influenced by the pleasure principle. You begin to rise above the distortions of subjective factors, like an aeroplane emerging from the clouds into the clear blue sky. You begin to see conditioned existence spread out, as it were, below you, its essential patterns becoming more apparent. You begin to see it as it is. Now you're in some degree clear of it, to some extent free of it, you can see it much more objectively. You begin to see things as they really are. You begin to see Reality. In other words, you develop at least the beginnings of Insight, or Wisdom, which leads directly to Enlightenment.

The word meditation clearly covers a great deal of ground, operating as it does on these three very different levels. The first level is concentration, really, rather than meditation; the second is meditation proper; and the third is contemplation. Being realistic, we have to say that most people are going to be occupied for a very considerable time with the first two: meditation as concentration and meditation as meditation. To start with, you simply want to integrate all your scattered energies. You want to pull yourself together; you want to be one person, not a number of conflicting selves. You don't want to waste your energies in internal and external discord; you want to be whole and harmonious. Only in that way can you deploy your energies effectively and be really happy.

When you have achieved this concentration of energies, the next step is to raise your consciousness above the usual – what we like to think of as our 'normal' – level. Here, in fact, you come to the nitty-gritty of meditation and the spiritual life: the transformation of consciousness. The point has already been made that we are embodiments of energy. It could equally well be said that we are embodiments of consciousness. We are what our state of consciousness is; our state of consciousness is us. So in the course of our spiritual life in general, and our meditation practice in particular, we are concerned with changing our state of consciousness – and it's not easy. Not only is it not easy – it is, for those who are not spiritually gifted from the beginning, very, very difficult. There are all sorts of hindrances, obstacles – plenty of exterior ones, obviously, but there are even more obstacles in our own mind, our own present state of conditioned consciousness. These hindrances, these obstacles, which prevent us from rising to a higher state of conscious-ness, the Buddhist tradition summarizes under the general heading of the five 'poisons' or 'defilements'. Strong words, perhaps, but the fact is that they defile and poison the whole of our existence, and, if we're not careful, even bring about our spiritual death.

The five poisons are distraction, aversion, craving, ignorance, and conceit, and for each of them there is an antidote in the form of a specific method of meditation. So if one particular poison predominates in us, we need to concentrate on the meditation practice which remedies that poison. If we find that one particular poison is predominant one week and another the next, we can change our method of practice accord-ingly. The five 'antidotes' are the five basic methods of meditation – one of which, as we shall see, is the recollection of death.

From the point of view of meditation, however, the first and funda-mental practice to undertake, without which any other practice will prove heavy going, is one that counters the poison of distraction. Particularly is this the case under the conditions of modern life: tech-niques of attention-grabbing seem to be brought to a fresh pitch of sophistication with every year that passes. So you're trying to do something, but your attention is taken away. Almost anything you see or hear seems capable of starting some train of thought or action which seems all the more inviting when you have set yourself to do something requiring a bit of concentration. Sometimes it seems practically impossible just to settle down and concentrate on one thing at a time. Someone can come to the door and you forget all about what you were supposed to be doing. What you find is that there's always some fascinating distraction on hand to drag your attention away – if it needs to be dragged. In fact, what seems to be presented as an unwilling submission to some irresistible outside force – 'I was distracted' – is actually a condition of one's own mind.

This inability to concentrate is very much to do with non-integration. Because one's energies are not all pulling in the same direction, it is impossible for one stream of energy, of volitional consciousness, to decide to concentrate on something without another part of oneself popping up and taking an interest in something else entirely. We become distracted when, after a struggle, the first self succumbs and the second self takes over. As far as the first self is concerned, the mind has wandered and one has become distracted. If anything is left of the first self it is just a nagging sense of unease.

The antidote to all this is simple. It lies in the method of meditation called the mindfulness of breathing. Through the various stages of this practice one's concentration on the natural rhythm of one's own breathing gradually gets deeper and more subtle. One gets more and more absorbed in the flow of the breath until eventually the breath seems to disappear, and one is just concentrated without concentrating on anything. The mind is just like a sphere resting on one non-dimensional point – perfectly at rest and perfectly mobile at the same time. With regular practice of this meditation technique one gains some measure of control over what one is doing. One also finds that the ability to put the whole of one's energies behind doing one thing at a time is the source of a relaxed and happy state of mind.

Having made some impression on the poison of distraction, we are now equipped to make some impression on the others. So the next one is aversion, or hatred. This is overcome by the practice of the *mettā bhāvanā*. *Bhāvanā* simply means 'development', but *mettā* is more difficult to translate, since there is nothing really like it in the English language. The usual translation is 'universal loving-kindness'. With this technique of meditation, the development of universal loving-kindness, one works to cultivate an attitude of positive emotion towards all living beings – a disposition towards feelings of friendliness, love, compassion, sympathy, and so on.

Like the mindfulness of breathing, the mettā bhāvanā proceeds through a number of stages. Starting by establishing a warm, positive regard for yourself, you then explore and connect with the feelings you have towards a good friend. In the context of the affectionate interest you have for your friend, you bring to mind someone for whom ordinarily you have very little feeling. When you have found you are able to experience genuine concern for this individual as well, you go on to extend this sense of care and goodwill to include someone you don't like. Finally, you establish the non-exclusivity of your sympathy and fellow-feeling by finding it in your heart to feel a real sense of kindness, of mettā, towards everyone, whoever and wherever they are – and indeed, towards all living beings. This practice is not about thinking vaguely beautiful thoughts. The aim is the cultivation of powerful, focused, precise positive emotion, as an antidote to a specific and powerful poison: aversion or hatred.

The third poison is craving. This is intense, neurotic desire: lust to possess this, that, and the other. It is a primordial, cardinal defilement, very difficult to overcome. Perhaps in recognition of the power it wields over us, not one but three meditation methods are prescribed as antidotes. First, the recollection of impurity. This is a rather drastic method that very few people have recourse to nowadays. It's usually supposed to be practised only by monks and hermits – people of this sort – rather than lay-folk; and in any case it calls for rather special facilities, to which not many people have access. The practice consists in going to a burning ground – one of the Indian type, with corpses and bones strewn everywhere – and contemplating cadavers in different stages of decay. This meditation is still practised by some people in the East, but obviously you need strong nerves and a strong spiritual resolution to be able to do it.

The second method of dealing with craving is the same sort of thing, only milder. This is the recollection of death, which must be undertaken on a firm foundation of mindfulness and emotional positivity, When you take up the practice of the recollection of death, your mind must already be relatively free of discursive thought, integrated, peaceful, harmonious, and happy – conditions you can most effectively establish with the help of the mindfulness of breathing and the mettā bhāvanā meditation practices. If you don't do this, the recollection of death meditation can even be harmful.

If, for instance, without being aware of how you were really feeling, or mindful of what you were doing, you began the practice by thinking of people near and dear to you who had died, you might start feeling sad – not in the positive sense of an objective sorrow, real compassion – but simply depressed; which is not the point of it at all. Or if, on the other hand, you happened to think of somebody you disliked who had died, you might find yourself feeling faintly pleased, thinking 'Well, thank goodness he's gone!' – which would also do more harm than good. Then again, you might bring to mind people who had died, or who were undergoing death, and feel a certain indifference about them – indifference not in the positive sense of equanimity, but in the sense of uncaring insensibility. This too would vitiate the practice.

Therefore, to avoid feelings of depression or *schadenfreude* or simple indifference, one is very strongly advised to start this practice in a mindful and positive frame of mind – if possible, in a higher state of consciousness, a state of serenity and happiness. And then you start reflecting that death is inevitable. This is a truism, of course, but though one may acknowledge its truth at a certain superficial level, it is another matter to absorb it sufficiently deeply to realize its truth as pertaining to one's own, most personal interests. So you begin this practice by allowing a simple truism to percolate down through your mind: 'I'm going to die. Death is inevitable.' It's as simple as that.

Simple to say, but actually far from simple to realize. Other factors being equal, the younger you are, the more difficult it is. When you are very young, it's virtually impossible. You have the irrational feeling that you're going to go on living for ever and ever. You may see people dying all around you every day, but it may still not occur to you to apply the fact of death to your own self. You can't grasp it. You can't imagine it. It seems so absolutely remote, absurd, and ridiculous, this fact that you're going to die. But it is a fact, and the older you get, the more clearly you see it. And when you see it, you begin to see, too, that until now you had never seen it, you had never understood this simple fact at all.

So at the beginning of this practice this is all you do. In a serene, happy, concentrated frame of mind you just let the thought of death, the thought that you are going to die, sink in. You say to yourself 'I'm going to die,' or, more traditionally, and even more succinctly, 'death … death', like a sort of mantra. Again traditionally, it's said to be helpful actually to see dead bodies, but this tip must, as always, carry a health warning. It's no use looking at corpses if your mind is unconcentrated, not very calm, liable to depression, and so on. You've got to have not only steady nerves in the ordinary sense but real inner calm. Otherwise, if you start looking around for corpses, you can, such is the power of meditation, do yourself real damage.

In most Western countries, of course, there's little chance of catching a glimpse of a corpse anyway, never mind being able to sit down and contemplate one. But another, less extreme, option is to keep a skull by you. One of the reasons the Tibetans go in for skull cups and thighbone trumpets and ornaments made of human bone is to familiarize themselves with the idea of death by handling these bits of people who were once living and breathing and feeling and are now dead. So if you don't want to go the whole hog and contemplate a corpse, you can get hold of a skull, or even just a fragment of bone, as a constant reminder of death. Some people in the Buddhist East have malas, or rosaries, made up from human bone – they come in discs rather than round beads. But once again, there should be nothing morbid or ghoulish about this. The indispensable basis for meditating on mortality is a serene state of concentration.

The next step in the practice, if the simple methods so far described don't seem to be producing results in the way of deepening your awareness of death, is to start thinking systematically of the precariousness of human life. You reflect that all the time life is hanging by a thread, that its continuance depends on any one of a number of factors. For one thing, you need air. If you stopped breathing for more than a few minutes, you'd just die. You are totally dependent on that pair of bellows inside the chest called the lungs. If they stopped pumping air – finish. If all the air were suddenly sucked out of the room – end of story. In the same way, you are dependent on a certain degree of warmth. If the temperature went up a little, we would all die, quite quickly. If it went down a little, we would be dead in no time. If the Earth was to wander just a little out of its orbit, that would be the end, for all of us. Life is so precarious, so contingent, it's a marvel that anybody's alive at all. Every moment of our lives is a step on a tightrope over an abyss. It's so difficult to be alive, and yet we are alive – we've managed it somehow – so far.

Another challenging angle on the matter, which can bring home to us how close we are to slipping from that tightrope, is the reflection that there is no special set of conditions for death. It's not as though you die at night but you don't die during the day. There's no time of the day or night when you can say to yourself, 'Well, I'm safe for a bit now.' It isn't like that. You can die during the night or during the day. And it isn't that if you are young you can think 'I'm young, so I'm not going to die. I'll only die when I'm old.' No, you can die either when you're young or when you're old. You can die when you're sick or when you're healthy. You can die in your home or outside. You can die in your own country or in a foreign land. There is no set of conditions within which you can be sure that you are not going to die. Death doesn't abide by any conditions. There is nowhere you can go to escape it. There is no time at which you can be sure that, because of such-and-such conditions, you're not going to die at that particular instant. You never know. There's absolutely no barrier between you and death at any time, in any place. So this can be quite a sobering subject for reflection.

You can also reflect upon the fact that everybody has to die. Every single member of the human race, however great, however distinguished, however noble, however famous – they all have to die one day. All the great men and women of the past have gone this way, even the Buddha. And if even the Buddha himself had to die, then you can be sure that you yourself are not going to escape.

Implicit in the practice of the recollection of death is the idea of impermanence. However, you can, if you like, make this broader principle the subject of your meditation. This is the third practice for the overcoming of the poison or defilement of craving. The recollection of the impermanence of all things is the mildest of the three antidotes to craving, but if you are sensitive and imaginative enough it can have a powerful impact. In the end, you always have to gauge which meditation is most suitable to practise at any one time on the basis of individual temperament and mood. This one, the recollection of the impermanence of all things, should be fairly self-explanatory. Everything changes. Nothing lasts. Evidence of impermanence is around you all day, every day, if you look for it. Again, you just have to bring a calm and positive sense of awareness to the meditation. Gradually, as the fragility of things and their inevitable decay becomes apparent, so does the falsity of the perception underlying the craving to possess become more and more obvious.

The fourth basic method of meditation is the one designed to overcome the poison of ignorance. Ignorance here means not lack of intellectual knowledge, but lack of awareness, the refusal to see things as they really are. The meditation which overcomes this culpable ignorance is the contemplation of a formulation of the truth which we have already come across: the chain of conditioned co-production.

This consists of twelve nidānas or links. Between them they represent the whole process of the reactive mind as it operates throughout this life – and not only this life, but the past life, the present life, and the future life. Basically, this chain of conditioned co-production is a framework by means of which one can get some understanding of the process of birth, death, and rebirth.

To enumerate the twelve links briefly, first of all there's ignorance – this is where it all starts. In dependence on ignorance there arise samskāras or volitions. In dependence on volitions there arises consciousness. In dependence on consciousness there arises the whole psychophysical organism. In dependence on the psychophysical organism there arise the six organs of sense, one mental and five physical. In dependence on those six organs of sense there arises contact with an external world. In dependence on that contact with an external world there arise feelings of various kinds: pleasant, painful, and neutral. In dependence on pleasant feeling there arises thirst or craving for the repetition of that pleasant feeling. In dependence on that thirst or craving, there arises grasping – the attempt to hang on to the pleasant feeling, and the object that created it. In dependence on that grasping and clinging, there arises becoming, which is the whole process of psychological conditioning, the whole process of the reactive mind itself. In dependence on becoming, there arises birth. And in dependence on that, there arises decay and death, and further rebirth.

These are the twelve links in the chain of conditioned co-production. To do the meditation practice, you first have to learn them off by heart – in the original Pali and Sanskrit if you like, or in English translation – it doesn't really matter. Then, having first established yourself in a state of concentration, you say to yourself, 'In dependence on ignorance arise volitions. In dependence on volitions arises consciousness. In dependence on consciousness arises the psychophysical organism,...' and so on. However, you don't just repeat the words. You don't content yourself with merely understanding the formula in an intellectual sense. You try to see what is really happening – because it's happening to you, it's happening in you. It's your own reactive mind that you are studying with the help of this framework.

What goes on in your mind as you do the meditation might be something like this. As you say to yourself, 'ignorance, ignorance,' you see in your mind's eye, if you like, a sort of great, pitch-black darkness. This is the darkness of ignorance. No light. No awareness. Consciousness has not arisen. And as you ponder on this, you see emerging out of this darkness, arising in dependence upon this darkness and blindness and ignorance, various actions of will, various strivings and volitions. But you see that these volitions are dull and dim and blind because they emerge out of that darkness. In this way, you see very clearly in the meditation all sorts of unaware, blind, thoughtless actions arising out of the fundamental, primordial state of ignorance which is within oneself.

Then you see how, as those volitions stumble on, as they bump into this and that, they get a bit more sensitive, a bit more aware, and just a tiny glimmering of consciousness arises. You see the little seed of individuality, tiny, frail, and flimsy, and how it gradually develops into a psychophysical organism – into a mind and body. You see the psychophysical organism developing different senses – of reason, of sight, of hearing, and so on. Then, as the organism comes into contact with the world through those senses, you see it experiencing all sorts of sensations – some painful, some pleasurable. You see it shrinking away from the painful sensations and trying to hang on to the pleasant sensations, becoming attached to them, and finally enslaved by them – conditioned by them. This process goes on and on like a wheel rolling. And so the Wheel of Life takes another turn.

As you continue to meditate, you see how your own mind works in this way. You see how you experience sensations – sights, sounds, smells, tastes, feelings, thoughts – and react to them. You like this, you want more of it. You feel sad or angry when it's over. You don't like that, you want to avoid it – you even hate it. The more you can see your own psychological conditioning at work in this way, seeing it objectively at the same time that you are experiencing it subjectively, the more you become free from it. You become free from your own psychological conditioning to the extent you see it. You become aware to the extent that you see you are unaware. And you can do this with the help of the traditional formula of the twelve links of the chain of conditioned co-production. You can certainly achieve the same sort of results with the help of a more contemporary psychological analysis of the process, if that is more appealing. What is essential, however, is to be able to see that your mind is not spontaneous and creative, but merely reactive, machine-like, and unaware. It is through seeing this that you gradually free yourself of spiritual ignorance.

Until we have completely freed ourselves from ignorance in this way, our death is simply the prelude to our rebirth, which takes place on account of the residue of craving, aversion, and ignorance left in the individual stream of consciousness at the time of death. In other words, if you have died with your passions unexhausted, if there is something that you still want, if there is something for which you still crave, something to which you are still attached – whether it is spouse and family, or riches, or name and fame, or even Buddhism perhaps – then you will have to come back. You will be drawn back by the power of your desire into a new body and a fresh incarnation.

But in the course of spiritual practice, one is gradually able to eliminate these three poisons. Cravings are attenuated, aversion is abated, ignorance is dispelled. In the end there is only a state of peace, a state of love, a state of wisdom. One is no longer bound to the Wheel. One no longer has to come back. When one dies, when the consciousness slips out – or flashes out – of the physical body, there is nothing to draw it back. It remains on the higher, archetypal, even transcendental plane of existence. It remains in nirvāṇa, the state of undisturbed Buddhahood. In other words, there is no need for any further rebirth.

At this point, according to Mahāyāna Buddhism, two possibilities, two different paths, disclose themselves. Having got this far, one alternative is just to remain there. One can allow oneself to disappear into nirvāṇa, to disappear from the ken of the world, slipping into nirvāṇa like 'the dewdrop ... into the shining sea.'[27] Or, on the other hand, one can turn back and decide quite voluntarily to be reborn – not because there is any residue of karma left unaccounted for, but out of compassion, so that one can continue to help other living beings in the world through the spiritual experience which one has gained.

This is the sort of story told, for instance, about the great Bodhisattva Avalokiteśvara, whose name means 'the one who looks down' – looks down, that is to say, in compassion. It is said that many, many centuries ago, Avalokiteśvara was a monk, a yogi, who practised meditation in a cave in the Himalayas for many years – in fact, for the greater part of his life. Then at last a moment came when he found himself on the very brink of Enlightenment. He ascended from one stage of superconsciousness to another, going farther and farther and farther away from the world. He passed through all sorts of archetypal, paradisal realms, and saw all sorts of glorious figures. Then all these experiences faded away, and he came to the shore, to the boundary, of a great ocean of light. He could see and hear nothing but this ocean of light, and he experienced tremendous joy and happiness that at last he was returning to his source, returning to his origins, and was going to be merged with Reality itself. With a great sigh of relief, he started to let himself go, to slip into that ocean of light.

But at that very moment, we are told, he heard a sound, a faint sound which seemed to be coming from a very long way away. At first he didn't know what it was, but it arrested his attention, and he began to listen. As he listened, the sound became a texture of but many sounds. He heard many voices, and they were all crying out, wailing, weeping, lamenting, grieving. The sound seemed to get louder and louder, until at last he turned his eyes away from the great ocean of light and looked down. He looked down right into the depths, right down to this world. And he saw in this world many people, millions of living beings, suffering in various ways due to their spiritual ignorance. Then the thought came to him, 'How can I leave these beings? How can I allow myself to merge into this ocean of light, just saving myself, when in the world below there are so many beings who need my help and guidance?' He turned back. He not only looked down – he *went* down. He chose the path that led back into the world.

The option which Avalokiteśvara eschewed, the path of allowing oneself to be merged into nirvāṇa, is the path of the Arhant, the one who desires his or her own individual salvation. The path he took, the path back down into the world, is the path of the Bodhisattva, the one who desires not just his or her own emancipation, but the liberation and Enlightenment of all living beings. The Bodhisattva is not satisfied until he can gather all living beings in his arms and take them with him into Buddhahood.

The path of the Bodhisattva is traditionally regarded as being higher than that of the Arhant, but the distinction between the two paths is not as black and white as all that. In a sense the Bodhisattva path includes and contains the path of the Arhant because one must at least have the capacity to gain liberation for oneself and remain in nirvāṇa for one's renunciation of that to have any meaning or significance at all. Otherwise, following the Bodhisattva ideal can turn into a rationalization of one's attachment to the world. In fact, the Bodhisattva ideal was implicit in the Buddha's own experience of Enlightenment. The Buddha's decision to teach was a natural expression of the Enlightenment experience.

However, the Bodhisattva ideal is, as Marco Pallis observes,[28] the presiding idea of Tibetan Buddhism. For Tibetan Buddhists it is a real, living thing, and one which they take very seriously indeed. They believe strongly that there are living in the world people who have made this great renunciation, this great sacrifice, people who have truly turned their backs on nirvāṇa and who have returned to the world to help in the higher evolution of humanity towards Enlightenment. For the Tibetans, the Bodhisattva ideal is a living reality.

It is on this sort of issue that religious differences cannot be judged. The view professed by a typical Roman Catholic commentator, for example, goes something like this: 'Well, the Bodhisattva ideal is very beautiful, but it's a beautiful dream. There are no Bodhisattvas in the world. The ideal of Christianity, the ideal of the crucified Christ, this is a historical reality. But the Bodhisattva ideal is just a sort of spiritual pipe-dream conjured up by the indolent Buddhist, lying on his couch in the East with nothing better to do than dream beautiful spiritual dreams.'

But it isn't like that, certainly for Tibetan Buddhists. They regard Bodhisattvas as being very much with us, as being bound up with the spiritual economy of the world. They believe very strongly that there are Bodhisattvas living in the world, and that it is possible to identify them. Not only is it possible; it is standard practice. Tibetans take it as read that highly spiritually advanced teachers can direct their rebirth. When a *tulku* or incarnate lama dies, his disciples embark on a search for his new incarnation, the young child he has been reborn as. When the child is discovered (or rather the *tulku* is rediscovered) he is given the traditional education in the Dharma that enables him to take up his Bodhisattva activity from where he left off in his previous life. The most famous of these *tulkus* is of course the Dalai Lama, whom the Tibetans regard as a manifestation of Avalokiteśvara himself, and who is both the spiritual leader of Tibet and – *de jure* if not *de facto* – its temporal ruler. Through the centuries he has been reborn again and again to give his guidance to Tibet, the present Dalai Lama being the fourteenth in the lineage.

To be drawn back into rebirth, to continue to circle round in the Wheel of Life, not through the poisons of craving, hatred, and ignorance, but out of compassion, requires spiritual awareness in the highest degree. And this we can begin to develop – remembering that a journey of a thousand miles begins with a single step – through meditating on the chain of conditioned co-production.

The fifth and last poison is māna, 'conceit', sometimes translated as pride, but really more like high-mindedness, or even high-and-mightiness. Pride is having a strong sense of 'I', 'me', 'mine', so in overcoming it you need to attack the whole 'I' feeling, especially as applied to the body. The method of meditation by which you launch this attack is called the contemplation of the six elements – these being earth, water, fire, air, space, and consciousness.

You begin, once again, by generating a calm, happy state of concentration. Then, as you're sitting meditating, you start to think about the element earth, and try to get a feeling for what it is. '*Earth. Earth.*' It's everything solid, everything cohesive. You can think of all sorts of things in the objective world that are solid – natural things like trees and rocks, man-made things like houses and books – all this is the element earth. Then you think, 'Not only is there the element of earth in the external world; there is also earth in the internal world, the subjective world, which is me. My bones, my flesh – they are derivatives of the element earth. Where have my bones come from? Where has my flesh come from? Where has the earth element in me come from?' You remind yourself: 'It's come from the earth element outside me. It's not mine. I've borrowed it, I've taken it from the earth element outside myself for a short time and incorporated it into my own being, my own substance, my own body, but I'm not going to be able to keep it for ever. After a few decades, after a few years – maybe sooner, who knows? – I'll have to give it back. The earth element in my body will be resolved into the earth element in the objective world. So how can I say of that earth element that this is mine, how can I say of it that it is me? It isn't mine, it isn't me. I've got to give it back. So all right, I'll let it go. It's not me. I can't claim to possess it. I can't identify with it.'

In the same way you take the element water. '*Water. Water.*' The water element is in whatever is fluid, liquid, flowing. In the world outside you find it in rivers, you find it in oceans, streams, rain, dew; and within you there's also a water element: blood, bile, tears, and so on. And where have you got that water from? Obviously from outside – and when you die, it has to go back where it came from. It doesn't belong to you, it isn't you – so let it go, cease to identify with it.

'*Fire. Fire.*' The fire element in the external world is the sun, the source of all the warmth and light of the solar system. There's warmth in us too, but where does it come from? It comes from the fire element in the external world. So again you reflect: 'One day I will have to give it back. I can't hold on to it for long. When I die, I'll go cold. Heat will disappear, leave the body. The fire element in me which is at the moment doing all sorts of things in my body – digesting my food and so on (according to traditional Indian ideas) – is not really mine. It doesn't belong to me.

I can't identify with it. So let it go. Let the heat element in me go back to the heat element in the universe.'

'*Air. Air.*' You think, 'There's air in the external world, obviously – there's this atmosphere which envelops the whole earth – and then in me there's the breath of life, which I'm inhaling and exhaling all the time. But I've only borrowed it for a short while. It's not mine. A time will come when I'll breathe in and breathe out, breathe in, breathe out – and then I won't breathe in again. I'll be dead, and there won't be any more breath left in my body. I'll have rendered it back for the last time. I can't say of the air element in me that it's me or mine. So let it go. I won't identify with it.'

'*Space. Space.* The body made up of the first four elements, with which I identify myself, occupies space. When the earth element goes from my body, when the water element goes, when the fire element and the air element go, what will be left? Nothing at all. Just an empty me-shaped space. So what is to differentiate that me-shaped space from the surrounding space? Nothing at all.' The Indian tradition says that just as if you break a clay pot, the space inside the pot merges with the space outside it, so that there's no difference any more; just so, when the body disintegrates, the space which was occupied by your physical body merges back into the universal space. You don't exist any more, so how can you hang on to this physical body which at the moment occupies space? You can't. So let that space which you are occupying merge into the universal space.

Sixthly and lastly, '*Consciousness. Consciousness.*' There's the consciousness associated with your physical body. You might say, 'Even if I'm not earth, even if I'm not water, or fire, or air, or even space, surely I am consciousness?' But no. Even consciousness is borrowed. Even what you call your consciousness is a sort of reflection, a gleam, of a higher, more universal consciousness, which is you in a sense, yes, but in another sense is very definitely not you. It's like the relationship between the waking state and the dream state. When you're awake, you can think in terms of 'having' a dream, but when you're actually dreaming, where are 'you'? It's as though the dream is having you. Similarly, in the case of the higher dimension of consciousness which we identify with 'me', the consciousness is there, but the 'me' has to go. So even individuality in that 'I' sense goes. It's as though the lower consciousness has to merge itself in the higher consciousness – but being consciousness (or at least conscious) without thereby being destroyed. There is no loss of consciousness, but consciousness is no longer centred on the 'I'. At the same time, paradoxically, in another sense you were never more completely yourself.

So this is the contemplation of the six elements, designed to counter-act the poison of pride, and the last of the five basic meditation prac-tices. However, there is another meditation practice based on the six elements, or at least the first five of them, and it brings us back to where we began – the Buddha's *parinirvāṇa*. In this practice you visualize the five elements symbolized by different geometrical figures of different colours. First of all you visualize a great yellow cube. This represents earth. On top of the yellow cube, a great white sphere or globe, repre-senting water. Next, on top of the white sphere, a brilliant red cone or pyramid – fire. Then, balanced on the point of the cone or pyramid, a blue saucer-shape: that's air. Finally, in that saucer-shape is a golden flame, which symbolizes space, or ether. And if you like, the tip of the golden flame can be rainbow-coloured – it can end in a rainbow-like jewel – and that will be consciousness.

These are the geometrical symbols of the five or six elements, and when you arrange them in this order, one on top of another, they add up to something else: the stupa – and the meditation is therefore called the stupa visualization. The stupa is of particular significance in this context, because it was originally a funeral monument of a rather special kind. Sometimes it contained ashes, and sometimes these ashes were those of someone held in very great reverence. In Buddhist history and tradition, the stupa is especially associated with the *parinirvāṇa* of the Buddha. In fact, in early Buddhist art, the stupa is actually the symbol of the *parinirvāṇa* itself.

This symbolic representation of the Buddha is an interesting and significant feature of archaic stone carvings by Buddhist artists – and the stupa is just one of a rich iconographic series. Sometimes he is represented simply by a pair of footprints, but there are all sorts of other symbols. In the case of a treatment of the Buddha's birth, the place of the infant Buddha is taken by a lotus flower. Where you get Siddhārtha leaving home, going into the jungle in quest of truth, you see the horse charging out of the palace gate, but there's only an umbrella over the horse's back to indicate where the figure would be. In the scene of the Buddha's Enlightenment, you see the bodhi tree, you see the throne, but the throne is empty – or there may just be a trident representing the Three Jewels. In the scene of the Buddha's first discourse, there are the five monks listening, there is the seat of the teacher, there are deer around, but what the five monks are apparently listening to is a wheel, a *dharmacakra* – the Wheel of the Dharma. In other contexts the Buddha is represented by the bodhi tree under which he gained Enlightenment – so you would have, say, the figure of Māra, the evil one, raising his club against the Buddha, but with no sign of the Buddha's presence in the scene apart from the bodhi tree. And likewise, in the earliest depictions of the Buddha's *parinirvāṇa*, instead of the figure of the Buddha lying on the stone couch under the sāl trees which you see in the art of the later Chinese and Japanese traditions, there is just a stupa to represent the presence of the Buddha.

There is, of course, a reason for all this. The early Buddhists, it seems, felt very strongly that the Buddha is incommensurable, that he is unrepresentable, that he is transcendental. A Buddha's nature is beyond thought, beyond speech, beyond words. When you come to speak of it, all you can do is remain silent. When you are drawing or carving a scene from the Buddha's life, and you come to the Buddha himself, all you can do is leave an empty space, or just a symbol. You can't represent the Buddha; the Buddha is beyond representation.

Although later artists did feel able to represent the Buddha, symbols like the Wheel of the Dharma, the bodhi tree, and perhaps particularly the stupa, have remained potent expressions of Enlightenment. Stupas built in various architectural forms are distinctive parts of the landscape throughout the Buddhist East, and small ones cast in brass or turned in wood are often kept in their homes by Buddhists as a reminder that one day we must all give the elements which we think of as 'me' back to the universe. All of us – even the Buddha – must die.

9

WHO IS THE BUDDHA?

BY NOW WE KNOW A GOOD DEAL about the Buddha. We know that he was born in the Lumbinī garden, we know how he was educated, we know how he left home, how he gained Enlightenment at the age of thirty-five, how he communicated his teaching, how he founded his Sangha, and how, finally, he passed away. And there is a good deal more we could find out. The traditional biographies give us all the facts. We could find out the names of the Buddha's half-brothers and cousins, the name of the town where he was brought up, the name of the astrologer who came to see him as a baby. But although his life is fully documented, although we've got the whole story, does his biography really tell us who the Buddha was? Do we know the Buddha from a description of the life of Gautama the Buddha?

What do we mean by 'knowing' the Buddha anyway? In what sense, really, do we know anybody? Suppose you are told all about someone: where they live, what they do – the sort of things people always want to know about a person – how old they are, and so on. In some sense you have an answer to the question, 'Who is this person?' You know their social identity, their position in society. Gradually you can fill in any number of details – how tall they are, their accent, their background, their taste in food and music, their political affiliations and their religious beliefs. You can then say you know *about* this person. But however much you know *about* someone, you would not claim to *know* them until you'd met them, until you'd met them a few times, probably. You'd then know them *personally*. This deeper knowledge would, in fact, be based on a relationship, on communication: you know someone, properly speaking, when they also know you. Eventually you may claim to know this person very well.

But is it really so? Do you really know them? After all, it sometimes happens that we have to correct our evaluation of someone. Sometimes we are taken completely by surprise. They do something quite unexpected, quite 'out of character', and we say to ourselves, rather surprised and sometimes a little hurt, 'Well, I never would have expected them to do that. They're the last person I'd have thought would do that.' But they did it, and this shows how little we really know other people. We are not truly able to fathom the deepest springs of their action, their fundamental motivation. This happens even with those who are supposedly nearest and dearest to us. It's a wise child that knows its own father, as the saying goes – and it's a wise father or mother that knows his or her own child.

Particularly, perhaps, it is a wise husband that knows his own wife, and a wise wife that knows her own husband. Sometimes I've had the experience of meeting – separately – a husband and wife, each having come to talk to me about the other. And usually what happens is that each gives a picture of the other that I would never have recognized. The impression I've had is that neither really knows the other. It's as though the so-called closeness gets in the way, and what we know is not the other person to whom we are supposed to be so close, but only our own projected mental state, our own quite subjective reaction to that person. In other words, our ego gets in the way.

In order really to know another person we have to go much deeper than the ordinary level of communication – which means, in effect, that ordinary communication is not real communication at all. It's just the same when it comes to knowing the Buddha. We may know all the biographical facts about his life, but are we thereby any nearer really knowing the Buddha? Well, no. The question continues to arise: Who was the Buddha? This question has been asked since the very dawn of Buddhism. In fact, the first question that was put to the Buddha after his Enlightenment was, 'Who are you?'

Walking along the road one day, the Buddha met a brahmin called Doṇa. As he saw the Buddha in the distance, coming towards him, there was something about the approaching figure that stopped Doṇa dead in his tracks. There were plenty of singular-looking individuals walking about India at that time – Doṇa himself was one of them – but Doṇa could see that this individual coming towards him was somehow utterly different from anyone he had ever seen. The Buddha, after all, was just fresh from his Enlightenment. He was happy, serene, and joyful; there was a radiance about his whole being, as though a light were shining from his face.

As the Buddha drew near, Doṇa asked him, 'Who are you?' Not 'Lovely weather we're having,' or 'Where are you from?' but 'Who are you?' If you were standing at the bus stop waiting for the bus into town and someone came up and said, 'Who are you?' you'd probably think they were being rather impertinent, but in India, of course, it's different, and Doṇa could put this question without fear of giving offence. The point is that Doṇa was not asking who the Buddha was in social terms; he was not asking what sort of a human being the Buddha was. Doṇa was, in fact, wondering if this was really a human being at all that he was seeing.

The ancient Indians believed that the universe was stratified into various levels of existence. There were not just human beings and animals, as we tend to think. There were also gods and ghosts and *yakṣas* and *gandharvas* – all sorts of mythological beings – inhabiting a sort of multi-storey universe. The human plane was just one out of scores of planes of existence. Doṇa's first thought, therefore, impressed as he was by the appearance of the Buddha, was, 'This isn't a human being. He must be from – or on his way to – some other realm. Perhaps he's a sort of spirit.' So he asked the Buddha, 'Who are you? Would you be a *deva*?' – a *deva* being a god, a divine being, a sort of archangel. The Buddha simply said, 'No.' So Doṇa tried again. 'Are you a *gandharva*?' This creature is like a kind of celestial musician, a beautiful, singing, angelic figure. The Buddha again said, 'No.' 'Well,' said Doṇa, 'Are you a *yakṣa*?' A *yakṣa* is a sort of sublime spirit, rather a terrifying one, who lives in the jungle. But the Buddha rejected this designation as well. Then Doṇa thought, 'He must be a human being after all. That's strange.' So he asked, 'Are you a human being?' (the kind of question you could only ask in ancient India) and once again the Buddha said, 'No.' 'Well, that *is* odd,' Doṇa thought. 'If he isn't a *deva*, or a *gandharva*, or a *yakṣa*, or a human being, what on earth is he?' 'Who are you?' he asked, now even more wonderingly. 'If you are none of these things, who are you? What are you?'

The Buddha said, 'Those conditions (or, perhaps better, those psychological conditionings) on account of which I might have been described as a *deva* or a *gandharva* or a *yakṣa* or a human being have been destroyed. Therefore am I a Buddha.' It is, as we have seen, these conditioned mental attitudes, volitions, or karma formations as they are sometimes called, which according to Buddhism (and Indian belief in general) determine our rebirth, as well as our human condition here and now. The Buddha was free from all this, free from all conditioning, so there was nothing to cause him to be reborn as a god or a *gandharva*, or even a human being. Even as he stood before this Brahmin, therefore, he was not any of these things. His body might appear to be that of a man, but his mind, his consciousness, was unconditioned, and therefore he was a Buddha. As a Buddha he was a personification, so to speak – even, if you like, an incarnation – of the Unconditioned mind.

What Doṇa tried to do is what we all try to do when we meet something new. The human mind proceeds slowly, by degrees, from the known to the unknown, and we try to describe the unknown in terms of the known; which is fair enough so long as one is aware of the limitations of this procedure. And we may say that the limitations of this procedure are most pronounced when it comes to trying to know other human beings.

There always seems to be a basic tendency to want to put people in categories and think that we have thereby got them neatly pigeonholed. In India I have often been stopped in the road by someone just passing, who has said, 'What is your caste?' – without any sort of preamble. If they can't classify you according to caste, they don't know what to do with you. They don't know how to treat you. They don't know whether they can take water from your hand or not, whether they can get to know you or not, whether you might marry their daughter or not. All these things are very important, especially in southern India. In Britain people are much more indirect in their approach, but they try to worm out of you the same sort of information. They want to know what sort of job you've got (and perhaps from that they try to work out your income), they want to know where you were born, where you were educated, where you live now, and by taking these various sociological readings, they gradually narrow down the field, and think they've got you nicely pinned down.

So likewise, when Doṇa saw this majestic, radiant figure, and wanted to know who – or what – it was, he had at his disposal various labels – *gandharva*, *yakṣa*, *deva*, human being – and he tried to stick these labels on what he saw. But the Buddha wouldn't have it. His reply said, in effect, 'None of these labels fit. None of them apply. I'm a Buddha. I transcend all conditionings. I am above and beyond all this.'

Doṇa may have been one of the first to puzzle over the Buddha's nature, but he was certainly not the last. We have already come across four of the Fourteen Inexpressibles: whether the Buddha would exist after death, or not, or both, or neither. Although the Buddha was constantly being asked about this – the ancient Indians had a real thing about it – he would always say that it was inappropriate to apply any of those four statements to a Buddha. And he would go on to say, 'Even during his lifetime, even when he sits there in a physical body, the Buddha is beyond all your classifications. You can't say anything about him.'[29]

This point is easily made, of course, but actually very difficult to accept, and it evidently needed to be constantly hammered home. The most suggestive and evocative repudiation of any attempt to grasp the nature of the Buddha is found in the *Dhammapada*: 'Whose conquest is not to be undone, whom not even a bit of those conquered passions follows, that Enlightened One whose sphere is endless, by what path will you trace him, the pathless one?'[30] According to this well-known verse, therefore, there is absolutely nothing by which a Buddha can be identified or tracked down or classified or categorized. You cannot trace the path of a bird's flight by looking for signs of its passage in the sky – and you cannot track a Buddha either.

If this is clear, however, it has not really been understood. It is somehow the nature of the human mind to keep on trying, and to imagine that, having understood what is being said, it understands what it is that is being spoken of. So if we turn to the *Sutta Nipāta*, we find the Buddha saying:

There is no measuring of man,
Won to the goal, whereby they'd say
His measure's so: that's not for him.
When all conditions are removed,
All ways of telling are removed.[31]

When all psychological conditions are removed in a person, you have no way of accounting for that person. You can't say anything about the Buddha because he doesn't have anything. In a sense, he isn't anything. In fact, we are introduced in this sutta to an epithet for an Enlightened being which says just this. *Akiñcana*, usually translated as 'man of nought', is one who has nothing because he is nothing. And of nothing, nothing can be said.

Although many of the Buddha's disciples gained Enlightenment, and themselves went through the world leaving no trace, as it were, they still worshipped the Buddha. They still felt there was something about him, about the man who discovered the Way for himself with no one to guide him, that was mysteriously beyond them and unfathomable. Even his chief disciple, Śāriputra, floundered when it came to estimating the Buddha's stature. He was once in the presence of the Buddha when, out of an excess of faith and devotion, he exclaimed, 'Lord, I think you are the greatest of all the Enlightened Ones who have ever existed, or will exist, or exist now. I think you are the greatest of them all.' The Buddha was neither pleased nor displeased by this. He didn't say, 'What a marvellous disciple you are, and how wonderfully well you understand me!' He just asked a question: 'Śāriputra, have you known all the Buddhas of the past?' Śāriputra said, 'No, Lord.' Then he said, 'Have you known all the Buddhas of the future?' 'No, Lord.' 'Do you know all the Buddhas that now are?' 'No, Lord.' Finally, the Buddha asked 'Do you even know me?' And Śāriputra said, 'No, Lord.' Then the Buddha said, 'That being the case, Śāriputra, how is it that your words are so bold and so grand?'[32]

So even the closest of his disciples didn't really know who the Buddha was. To try to make sense of this attitude, they put together, after his death, a list of ten powers and eighteen special qualities which they attributed to the Buddha just to distinguish him from his Enlightened disciples. But in a way this was just an expression of the fact that they simply could not understand who or what he was at all.

This fact that the Enlightened disciples of the Buddha, enjoying personal contact with him, did not understand who he really was does not say much for our own chances in the matter. However, at a certain level, we can build up a collection of hints and clues, and the episode with Doṇa offers an important lead. What it is suggesting is that we have to step back and bring in a whole new dimension to our search for the Buddha. He is untraceable because he belongs to a different dimension, the transcendental dimension, the dimension of eternity.

So far we have seen him very much in terms of time – his birth, his Enlightenment, his death – his historical existence. We have, in fact, been looking at him according to the evolutionary model we introduced in the first chapter, which model is, of course, one of progress through space and time. This, however, is only one way of looking at things. As well as looking at the Buddha from the standpoint of time, we can also look at him from the standpoint of eternity.

The problem with any biographical account of the Buddha is that in a sense it deals with two quite different people: Siddhārtha and the Buddha – divided by the central event of the Enlightenment. But one tends to come away from the biographical facts with the view that his early life simply built up to this point, and that after it he was more or less the same as he was before – apart from being Enlightened, of course. If we had been around at the time we should probably have been none the wiser. If we had known the Buddha a few months before he was Enlightened and a few months after, we should almost certainly not have been able to perceive any difference in him at all. We would have seen the same physical body, probably the same clothes. He spoke the same language and had the same general characteristics. This being so, we tend to regard the Buddha's Enlightenment as a finishing touch to a process which had been going on for a long time, the feather that turned the scale, the final piece of the jigsaw, that little difference that made all the difference. But really it isn't like that at all – not in the least like that.

Enlightenment – the Buddha's or anybody else's – represents 'the intersection of the timeless moment.'[33] We need to modify T.S. Eliot's analogy a little, because strictly speaking only a line can intersect another line, and although we can represent time as a line, the whole point of the timeless – eternity – is that it isn't a line. Perhaps we should think rather in terms of time as a line which at a given point just stops, just disappears into another dimension. It's rather like – to use a hackneyed but (if we don't take it too literally) rather useful simile – the flowing of a river into the ocean, where the river is time and the ocean is eternity. Perhaps, indeed, we can improve on the simile to some extent. Suppose we imagine that the ocean into which our river is flowing is just over the horizon. From where we are, we can see the river flowing to the horizon, but we can't see the ocean into which the river is flowing, so it seems as though the river is flowing into nothingness, flowing into a void. It just stops at the horizon because that is the point at which it enters the new dimension which we cannot see.

The point of intersection is what we call Enlightenment. Time just stops at eternity; time is succeeded, so to speak, by eternity. Siddhārtha disappears, like the river disappearing at the horizon, and the Buddha takes his place. This is, of course, from the standpoint of eternity. Whereas from the standpoint of time Siddhārtha *becomes*, evolves into, the Buddha, from the standpoint of eternity Siddhārtha just ceases to exist, and there is the Buddha, who has been there all the time.

This difference of approach – in terms of time and in terms of eternity – is at the bottom of the whole controversy between the two schools of Zen, the gradual school and the abrupt school. In the early days of Zen (or rather Ch'an) in China, there were two apparently opposing viewpoints: there were those who believed that Enlightenment was attained in a sudden flash of illumination; and there were those who believed that it was attained gradually, step by step, by patient effort and practice. In the *Platform Sūtra* Hui Neng tries to clear up the whole controversy: he says it isn't that there are two paths, a gradual one and a sudden one; it is merely that some people gain Enlightenment more quickly than others, presumably because they make a greater effort.

This is true, but you can go deeper than this. The abrupt attainment of Enlightenment, you may say, has nothing to do with speed within time. It doesn't mean that you begin the usual process of attaining Enlightenment and get through it more quickly. It doesn't mean that whereas you might normally spend fifteen or fifty years on the gradual path, you are somehow able to speed it up and compress it into a year, or even a month, or a week, or a weekend. The abrupt path is outside time altogether. Sudden Enlightenment is simply the point at which this new dimension of eternity outside time is entered. You can never get closer to eternity by speeding up your approach to it within time. Within time you just have to stop. At the same time, of course, you can't stop without first having speeded up. So Enlightenment can be looked at from two points of view, both of which are valid. It can be regarded as the culmination of the evolutionary process, a culmination which is reached through personal effort. But Enlightenment can also be regarded as being a sort of breakthrough into a new dimension beyond time and space.

There is a rather picturesque story which vividly illustrates the paradoxical meeting of these two dimensions. It concerns a famous bandit, called Aṅgulimāla, who lived in a great forest somewhere in northern India. Aṅgulimāla's speciality was to ambush travellers on their way through the forest, murder them, and chop off one of their fingers as a trophy. These fingers he strung into a garland which he wore round his neck; hence his name, Aṅgulimāla, meaning 'garland of fingers'. It was his ambition to have one hundred fingers on his garland, and he had got to ninety-eight when the Buddha happened to pass through that forest. The village folk had tried to dissuade him from entering it, warning him that he was in danger of losing a finger – and his life – to the notorious Aṅgulimāla, but the Buddha had carried on regardless. The sight of him just about made Aṅgulimāla's day, because he had been getting a bit desperate to find the last two fingers for his garland. His mother, a devoted old soul, was living with him in the forest and cooking for him, and he had got so fed up with waiting he had finally decided there was nothing for it but to add one of *her* fingers to his collection (maybe she used to nag him a bit). That would make ninety-nine, so he would just need one more. He had been on his way to find his poor old mother when he saw the Buddha coming through the forest. He thought, 'Well, I can always deal with mother later. But first I will settle the hash of this *śramaṇa*. Finger number ninety-nine coming up!'

It was a beautiful afternoon, a gentle breeze stirring the tree-tops and the birds singing, when the Buddha came walking along the little trail that wound through the forest. He walked meditatively, slowly, thinking to himself or, perhaps, not thinking at all. Aṅgulimāla emerged from the forest, and stealthily began to tail the Buddha, creeping up on him from behind. He had his sword drawn ready, so he could make very quick work of his prey when he got close to him. He loped along smoothly and rapidly to cut down the distance between them before he was seen. The last thing he wanted was a long messy struggle.

After he had followed the Buddha for a while, however, he noticed that something rather odd was happening. Although he seemed to be moving much more quickly than the Buddha, he didn't seem to be getting any closer to him. There was the Buddha way in front, pacing slowly, and there was Aṅgulimāla shadowing him and trying to catch up, but not getting any nearer. Aṅgulimāla quickened his pace, and then he was running, but he still got no nearer to the Buddha. When Aṅgulimāla realized what was happening, he apparently broke into a cold sweat of terror and astonishment and bewilderment. But he was not a man to give up easily – or to stop and think about things either. He just lengthened his stride till he was sprinting along in the wake of the Buddha. The Buddha, however, stayed just the same distance ahead, and if anything he seemed to be going even more slowly. It was like a bad dream.

In desperation, Aṅgulimāla called out to the Buddha: 'Stand still!' The Buddha turned round and said, 'I am standing still. It is you who are moving.' So Aṅgulimāla, who had considerable presence of mind despite his fear – for he was a bold fellow – said, 'You are supposed to be a *śramaṇa*, a holy man. How can you tell such a lie? Here am I running like mad, and I can't catch up with you. What do you mean, you are standing still?' The Buddha said, 'I am standing still because I am standing in nirvāṇa. I have come to rest. You are moving because you are going round and round in *saṁsāra*.'[34]

Of course, Aṅgulimāla becomes the Buddha's disciple, but that, and what happens afterwards, is another story. What this particular adventure illustrates is that Aṅgulimāla could not catch up with the Buddha because the Buddha was moving – or standing still, it is the same thing here – in another dimension. Aṅgulimāla, representing time, couldn't catch up with the Buddha, representing eternity. However long time goes on, it never comes to a point where it catches up with eternity. Time doesn't find eternity within the temporal process. Aṅgulimāla couldn't have caught up with the Buddha even if the Buddha had come to a dead halt. He could still be running now, after 2,500 years, but he still wouldn't have caught up with the Buddha.

When the Buddha attained Enlightenment, he entered a new dimension of being. There was no continuity, essentially, from the person who was there before. He was not just the old Siddhārtha slightly improved, or even considerably improved, but a new person. This is actually a very difficult thing to grasp, it needs reflecting on, because we naturally think of the Buddha's Enlightenment in terms of our own experience of life. In the course of our lives we may add to our knowledge, learn different things, do different things, go to different places, meet different people, life teaches us things – but underneath we remain fundamentally and recognizably the same person. Whatever changes take place don't go that deep. 'The child is father to the man' – that is, what one is now is determined to a remarkable degree by what one was as a child. One remains much the same person as one was then. The conditions for one's fundamental attitude to life were set up a long time ago, and any change that takes place subsequently is comparatively superficial. This even applies to our commitment to a spiritual path. We may take to Buddhism, we may 'go for Refuge' to the Buddha, but the change isn't usually very deep.

But the Buddha's experience of Enlightenment wasn't like that. In reality it wasn't an experience at all, because the person to have the experience wasn't there any more. The 'experience' of Enlightenment is therefore more like death. It is more like the change that takes place between two lives, when you die to one life and are reborn in another. In some Buddhist traditions Enlightenment is called 'the great death', because everything of the past dies, everything, in a way, is annihilated, and you are completely reborn. In the case of the Buddha, it is not that he was a smartened up version of Siddhārtha, Siddhārtha tinkered about with a bit, Siddhārtha reissued in a new edition. Siddhārtha was finished. At the foot of the bodhi tree Siddhārtha died and the Buddha was born – or we should say, rather, that he 'appeared'. At that moment, when Siddhārtha dies, the Buddha is seen as having been alive all the time – by which we really mean above and beyond time, out of time altogether.

Even to talk in this way is again misleading, because it is not as if, being outside time, you are really outside anything. Time and space are not things in themselves. We usually think of space as a sort of box within which things move about, and time as a sort of tunnel along which things move – but they are not really like that. Space and time are really forms of our perception. We see things through the spectacles, as it were, of space and time. And we speak of these things that we see as phenomena – which are, of course, what make up the world of relative, conditioned existence, or saṃsāra. So what we call phenomena are only realities as seen under the forms of space and time. But when we enter the dimension of eternity, we go beyond space and time, and therefore we go beyond the world, we go beyond saṃsāra, and, in the Buddhist idiom, we enter nirvāṇa.

Enlightenment is often described as awakening to the truth of things, seeing things as they really are, not as they appear to be. The Enlightened person sees things free from any veils or obscurations, sees them without being influenced or affected by any assumptions or psychological conditionings, sees them with perfect objectivity – not only sees them, but becomes one with them, one with the reality of things. So the Buddha, the one who has awoken to the Truth, the one who exists out of time in the dimension of eternity, may be regarded as Reality itself in human form. This is what is meant by saying that the Buddha is an Enlightened human being: the form is human, but in the place, so to speak, of the conditioned human mind, with all its prejudices and preconceptions and limitations, there is Reality itself, there is an experience or awareness which is not separate from Reality.

In the Buddhist tradition this crystallized eventually into a very important distinction which came to be established with regard to the Buddha. On the one hand there was his *rūpakāya* (literally 'form body'), his physical phenomenal appearance; on the other, there was, or rather *is*, his *dharmakāya* (literally 'body of Truth' or 'body of Reality'), his true, his essential, form. The *rūpakāya* is the Buddha as existing in time, but the *dharmakāya* is the Buddha as existing out of time in the dimension of eternity. Wherein lies the true nature of the Buddha, in his *rupakāya* or his *dharmakāya*, is declared definitively in a chapter from one of the great Perfection of Wisdom texts, the *Diamond Sūtra*. In it the Buddha says to his disciple, Subhūti:

> *Those who followed me by voice,*
> *Wrong the effort they engaged in.*
> *Me those people will not see.*
> *From the Dharma should one see the Buddhas,*
> *From the Dharma-bodies comes their guidance.*
> *Yet Dharma's true nature cannot be discerned,*
> *And no one can be conscious of it as an object.*[35]

The Buddha is found to be equally emphatic on this point in the Pali canon. Apparently there was a monk called Vakkali who was very devoted to the Buddha, but his devotion had got stuck at a superficial level. He was so fascinated by the appearance and the personality of the Buddha that he used to spend all his time sitting and looking at him, or following him around. He didn't want any teaching. He didn't have any questions to ask. He just wanted to look at the Buddha. So one day the Buddha called him and said, 'Vakkali, this physical body is not me. If you want to see me, you must see the Dharma, you must see the *dharmakāya*, my true form.'[36] So Vakkali meditated on this, and he gained liberation by meditating in this way very shortly before he died.

Vakkali's problem is actually one that most of us have. It's not that we should ignore the physical body, but we should take it as a symbol of the *dharmakāya*, the Buddha as he is in his ultimate essence. That said, it must be admitted that the word Buddha is ambiguous. When, for instance, we say, 'The Buddha spoke the language of Magadha,' we are obviously referring to Gautama the Buddha, the historical figure. On other occasions, however, 'Buddha' means the transcendental Reality, as when we say, 'Look for the Buddha within yourself.' Here we don't mean Gautama the Buddha; we mean the eternal, time-transcending Buddha-nature within ourselves. Broadly speaking, the Theravāda School today uses the word Buddha more in the historical sense, whereas the Mahāyāna, especially Zen, tends to use it more in the spiritual, trans-historical sense.

The shifting usage of this word only adds to the confusion Westerners are liable to feel when it comes to identifying the Buddha. Like Doṇa, we want to know who the Buddha is, we want to slap a label on him. But with our Western, dualistic, Christian background we have only two labels available to us: God and Man. Some people tend to say that the Buddha was just a man – a very good man, a very holy man, very decent, but just a man, no more than that. He's someone rather like Socrates. This is the view taken, for instance, by Catholic writers about Buddhism. It's a rather subtle, insidious approach. They praise the Buddha for his wonderful piety, wonderful charity, great love, compassion, wisdom – yes, he's a very great man. Then, on the last page of their book about Buddhism, they carefully add that of course the Buddha was just a man, and not to be compared with Christ, who was, or is, the son of God. This is one way in which the Buddha gets misplaced. The other way people fail to see him is by saying, 'No, the Buddha is a sort of god for the Buddhists. Of course, he was originally a man, but then, hundreds of years after his death, those misguided Buddhists went and made him into a god, because they wanted to have something to worship.'

Both these views are wrong, and the source of this misconception probably lies in a general misunderstanding of what religion is necessarily about. People for whom the idea of a non-theistic religion is a contradiction in terms will always want to resolve the question of how the Buddha stands in relation to God. Christ is said by his followers to be the son of God. Muhammad is supposed to be the messenger of God. The Jewish prophets claim to be inspired by God. And Krishna and Rama are claimed to be incarnations of God. Indeed, many Hindus think of the Buddha as one as well. They look upon him as the ninth incarnation, the ninth *avatar*, of the god Vishnu. This is how they see him because the category of *avatar* is a familiar one to them. But neither the Buddha nor his followers make any such claim, because Buddhism is a non-theistic religion. Like some other religions – Taoism, Jainism, and certain forms of philosophical Hinduism – in Buddhism there is no place for God *at all*. There is no supreme being, no creator of the universe, and there never has been. So Buddhists can worship as much as they like, but they will never be worshipping their creator or any conception of a personal God.

The Buddha is neither man nor God, nor even a god. He was a human being in the sense that he started off as every other human being starts off, but he didn't remain an ordinary human being. He became an Enlightened human being, and according to Buddhism that makes a great deal of difference – in fact, all the difference. He was an Unconditioned mind in a conditioned body. According to the Buddhist tradition, a Buddha is the highest being in all the universe, higher even than the so-called gods (whom in Western terms we would call angels, archangels, and so on). Traditionally the Buddha is called the teacher of gods and men, and in Buddhist art the gods are represented in a very humble position, saluting the Buddha and listening to his teaching. Therefore there is no possibility, whether on a philosophical or a popular level, of confusing the Buddha with any kind of god.

For those of us brought up to imagine that if anyone is the highest being in the universe that person is God, it is not so easy to really discern the Buddha in that position. Even if we don't believe in God, we see a God-shaped empty space, and the Buddha simply does not measure up to it. After all, he has not created the universe. We see the Buddha in this way because there's a category missing, we may say, from Western thought. If, therefore, we are to perceive who the Buddha is we have to dispel the ghost of God, the creator of the universe that looms over him, by substituting for God something completely different.

After all this, are we any nearer to answering the question, 'Who is the Buddha?' We've seen that Buddha means Unconditioned mind, Enlightened mind. Knowing the Buddha therefore means knowing the mind in its Unconditioned state. So the answer to the question 'Who is the Buddha?' is really that we ourselves are the Buddha – potentially. We really, truly come to know the Buddha only in the course of our spiritual life, in the course of our meditation, in the course of actualizing our own potential Buddhahood. It is only then that we can really say, from knowledge and experience, who the Buddha is.

We can't do this all at once. It certainly can't be done in a day. First of all we have to establish a living contact with the Buddha. We have to arrive at something intermediate between mere factual *knowledge* about Gautama the Buddha – the details of his career – and on the other hand, the *experience* of Unconditioned mind. This intermediate stage is what we call Going for Refuge to the Buddha. And it means not just reciting '*Buddhaṁ saraṇaṁ gacchāmi*' ('to the Buddha for Refuge I go'), though it doesn't exclude that. It means committing ourselves to the goal of Enlightenment as a living ideal, as our ultimate objective, and striving to realize it. It is only by Going for Refuge to the Buddha, with all that this implies, with all that this means, that we can answer from the heart and the mind and the whole of our spiritual life the question: 'Who is the Buddha?'

NOTES AND REFERENCES

1   'The English Flag'

2   The issue of the 'two cultures', first debated by T.H. Huxley and Matthew Arnold in 1881–2, came to a head in a crusty confrontation between C.P. Snow and F.R. Leavis in 1959.

3   'Ode to Melancholy'

4   *Vinaya Cuḷavagga* x.5

5   *Saṁyutta Nikāya* ii.104

6   *Jātaka* i.60; *Dhammapadaṭṭhakatā* i.70

7   The story of the Four Sights is told in Aśvaghoṣa's*Buddhacarita*, canto iii, and at *Mahāvastu* ii.150.

8   Shakespeare, 'The Tempest', act i, scene ii

9   *Dhammapada* 103

10 *Buddhacarita* xii.120; *Lalitavistara* 19

11 e.g. *Majjhima Nikāya* i.118; *Saṁyutta Nikāya* iv.133

12 sGam.po.pa, *The Perfection of Wisdom in Eight Thousand Lines*, trans. Edward Conze, Four Seasons, Bolinas 1973, pp.223–4

13 *Vinaya Cūḷavagga* 7.3.1

14 *Saṁyutta Nikāya*.i.139

15 *Cūḷavedalla Sutta, Majjhima Nikāya* 44

16 Alexander Pope, *Satires, Epistles, and Odes of Horace*, satire i, book ii (1740)

17 *Saṁyutta Nikāya*.i.137

18 The commentators on this verse interpret 'release their faith' in two different ways. It could mean 'let them let go of their wrong faith,' i.e. let them give up their faith in teachings that do not lead to Enlightenment. But it could also mean 'let them release their right faith,' i.e. let them free up their faith in teachings that do lead to Enlightenment.

19 *Saṁyutta Nikāya* v.2

20 The Buddha is widely referred to by this title, which literally translates as 'Thus-come' or 'Thus-gone', so it means one who has 'gone beyond' conditioned existence – who leaves no trace.

21 A *śramaṇa* is someone who has taken up a homeless religious life.*Śramaṇa* literally means 'one who is washed, purified,' and it shares this literal meaning with the words 'Sufi' and 'Cathar'. The quotation is from*Vinaya Mahāvagga* i.23.

22 Thomas Gray, 'Elegy in a Country Churchyard', 1750

23 'Burnt Norton', *Four Quartets*, 1944

24 *Saṁyutta Nikāya* iii.257

25 *Mahāparinibbāna Sutta, Digha Nikāya* 16.2.26

26 *Mahāparinibbāna Sutta, Digha Nikāya* 16.6.7

27 The last line of *The Light of Asia*, by Edwin Arnold

28 *Peaks and Lamas*

29 e.g. *Saṁyutta Nikāya* iii.118–9; *Majjhima Nikāya* i.140

30 *Buddhavagga* verse 1

31 *Sutta Nipāta* v.6 (1076), *Upasīvamānavapucchā*

32 *Mahāparinibbāna Sutta, Digha Nikāya* 16.1.16

33 *Here, the intersection of the timeless moment*
    Is England and nowhere. Never and always.
        'Little Gidding', *Four Quartets*, 1944

34 *Aṅgulimāla Sutta, Majjhima Nikāya* 86

35 *Diamond Sūtra* xxvi

36 *Saṁyutta Nikāya* iii.120

Further Reading

E. Arnold, *The Light of Asia*, Windhorse Publications, Birmingham 1999

G. Bays, *The Voice of the Buddha (Lalitavistara)*, Dharma, Berkeley USA 1983

M. Carrithers, *The Buddha*, Oxford University Press, Oxford 1983

E. Conze, *A Short History of Buddhism*, Allen and Unwin, London 1980

D.W. Evans, *Discourses of Gotama Buddha*, Janus, London 1992.

Z. Ishigami (ed.), *Disciples of the Buddha*, Kosei, Tokyo 1989

Jinananda, *Warrior of Peace*, Windhorse Publications, Birmingham 2002

E.H. Johnstone, *The Buddhacarita*, Motilal Banarsidass, Delhi 1992

L.M. Joshi, *Discerning the Buddha*, Munshiram Manoharlal, New Delhi 1983

D.J.I. Kalupahana, *The Way of Siddhartha*, University Press of America, New York 1987

T. Ling, *The Buddha's Philosophy of Man*, Everyman's Library, London 1981

Bhikkhu Ñāṇamoli, *The Life of the Buddha*, Buddhist Publication Society, Sri Lanka 1992

K.R. Norman (trans.), *The Sutta Nipāta*, Pali Text Society, London 1992

M. Pye, *The Buddha*, Duckworth, London 1979

Saddhaloka, *Encounters With Enlightenment*, Windhorse Publications, Birmingham 2001

H. Saddhatissa, *The Life of the Buddha*, Allen and Unwin, London 1976

Sangharakshita, *The Buddha's Victory*, Windhorse Publications, Glasgow 1991

H.W. Schumann, *The Historical Buddha*, Arkana, London 1989

M. Walshe (trans.), *The Long Discourses of the Buddha (Dīgha Nikāya)*, Wisdom, Boston 1995

INDEX

WINDHORSE PUBLICATIONS

Windhorse Publications is a Buddhist charitable company based in the UK. We place great emphasis on producing books of high quality that are accessible and relevant to those interested in Buddhism at whatever level. We are the main publisher of the works of Sangharakshita, the founder of the Triratna Buddhist Order and Community. Our books draw on the whole range of the Buddhist tradition, including translations of traditional texts, commentaries, books that make links with contemporary culture and ways of life, biographies of Buddhists, and works on meditation.

As a not-for-profit enterprise, we ensure that all surplus income is invested in new books and improved production methods, to better communicate Buddhism in the 21st Century. We welcome donations to help us continue our work - to find out more, go to www.windhorsepublications.com.

The Windhorse is a mythical animal that flies over the earth carrying on its back three precious jewels, bringing these invaluable gifts to all humanity: the Buddha (the 'awakened one') his teaching, and the community of all his followers.

Windhorse Publications	Perseus Distribution	Windhorse Books
169 Mill Road	1094 Flex Drive	PO Box 574
Cambridge CB1 3AN UK	Jackson TN 38301	Newtown NSW 2042
info@windhorsepublications.com	USA	Australia

TRIRATNA BUDDHIST COMMUNITY

Windhorse Publications is a part of the Triratna Buddhist Community, which has more than sixty centres on five continents. Through these centres, members of the Triratna Buddhist Order offer classes in meditation and Buddhism, from an introductory to deeper levels of commitment. Bodywork classes such as yoga, Tai chi, and massage are also taught at many Triratna centres. Members of the Triratna community run retreat centres around the world, and the Karuna Trust, a UK fundraising charity that supports social welfare projects in the slums and villages of South Asia.

Many Triratna centres have residential spiritual communities and ethical Right Livelihood businesses associated with them. Arts activities are encouraged too, as is the development of strong bonds of friendship between people who share the same ideals. In this way Triratna is developing a unique approach to Buddhism, not simply as a set of techniques, but as a creatively directed way of life for people living in the modern world.

If you would like more information about Triratna please visit www.thebuddhistcentre.com or write to:

London Buddhist Centre	Aryaloka	Sydney Buddhist Centre
51 Roman Road	14 Heartwood Circle	24 Enmore Road
London E2 0HU	Newmarket NH 03857	Sydney NSW 2042
UK	USA	Australia

Also from Windhorse Publications

Buddhist Wisdom in Practice series

The Art of Reflection

by Ratnaguna

It is all too easy either to think obsessively, or to not think enough. But how do we think usefully? How do we reflect? Like any art, reflection can be learnt and developed, leading to a deeper understanding of life and to the fullness of wisdom. *The Art of Reflection* is a practical guide to reflection as a spiritual practice, about "what we think and how we think about it". It is a book about contemplation and insight, and reflection as a way to discover the truth.

No-one who takes seriously the study and practice of the Dharma should fail to read this ground-breaking book. – Sangharakshita, founder of the Triratna Buddhist Community

ISBN 9781 899579 89 1
£9.99 / $16.95 / €11.95
160 pages

This Being, That Becomes

by Dhivan Thomas Jones

Dhivan Thomas Jones takes us into the heart of the Buddha's insight that everything arises in dependence on conditions. With the aid of lucid reflections and exercises he prompts us to explore how conditionality works in our own lives, and provides a sure guide to the most essential teaching of Buddhism.

Clearly and intelligently written, this book carries a lot of good advice. – Prof Richard Gombrich, author of *What the Buddha Thought*.

ISBN 9781 899579 90 7
£12.99 / $20.95 / €15.95
216 pages

The Three Jewels series

by Sangharakshita

This set of three essential texts introduces the Three Jewels which are central to Buddhism: the *Buddha* (the Enlightened One), the *Dharma* (the Buddha's teachings), and the *Sangha* (the spiritual community).

What Is the Dharma?: The Essential Teachings of the Buddha

Guided by a lifetime's experience of Buddhist practice, Sangharakshita tackles the question 'What is the Dharma?' from many different angles. The result is a basic starter kit of teachings and practices, which emphasizes the fundamentally practical nature of Buddhism.

In turn refreshing, unsettling, and inspiring, this book lays before us the essential Dharma, timeless and universal: the Truth that addresses the deepest questions of our hearts and minds and the Path that shows us how we can renew our lives.

264 pages
ISBN 9781 899579 01 3
£12.99 / $20.95 / €15.95

What Is the Sangha?: The Nature of Spiritual Community

Sangharakshita presents the ideal sangha as a free association between developing individuals. An exploration of the nature of spiritual community is balanced by reflections on individuality, on what it is to be truly human.

Sangha being all about relationships, this book also considers the individual's relationships to others – friends, family, fellow workers, and spiritual teachers – and the connections of the Buddhist community to the world as a whole.

288 pages
ISBN 1 899579 31 1
£9.99 / $19.95

Meeting the Buddhas series

by Vessantara

This set of three informative guides, by one of our best-selling authors, introduces the historical and archetypal figures from within the Tibetan Buddhist tradition. Each book focuses on a different set of figures and features full-colour illustrations.

A Guide to the Buddhas

ISBN 9781 899579 83 9
£11.99 / $18.95 / €18.95
176 pages

A Guide to the Bodhisattvas

ISBN 9781 899579 84 6
£11.99 / $18.95 / €18.95
128 pages

A Guide to the Deities of the Tantra

ISBN 9781 899579 85 3
£11.99 / $18.95 / €18.95
192 pages